Justice in a Changing World

Justice in a Changing World

Cécile Fabre

polity

First published in 2007 by Polity Press.

Polity Press
65 Bridge Street
Cambridge CB2 1UR, UK

Polity Press
350 Main Street
Malden, MA 02148, USA

ISBN-13: 978-07456-3969-7
ISBN-13: 978-07456-3970-3 (pb)

A catalogue record for this book is available from the British Library.

Typeset in 11 on 13 pt Scala
by Servis Filmsetting Ltd, Manchester
Printed and bound in India by Replika Press Pvt Ltd.

For further information on Polity, visit our website: www.polity.co.uk

Contents

Acknowledgements

This book began as two different series of lectures I gave at the London School of Economics between 2001 and 2006. Before assuming its present shape, it became a course guide for the University of London's external degree programme. Turning lecture notes into a coherent text has proved much harder than I had anticipated. I am grateful to Kate Barker, the administrator of the programme, and to Iain Sharpe, who copy-edited the guide, for their encouragement and support. Likewise, I would not have found the energy to expand the lectures and the course guide into a book had it not been for Louise Knight's commitment to the project. She and her team at Polity Press (most notably Caroline Richmond) have been a remarkable and steadfast fountain of advice, ranging from the academic to the editorial. Axel Gosseries and Andrew Williams helped with future generations; Dan Butt, Clare Chambers, Nicola Dunbar, Paul Kelly, and Phil Parvin read parts of the typescript and provided advice of various kinds; Matthew Festenstein and an anonymous reader for Polity Press helped me knock the whole thing into shape.

This book differs somewhat from other well-known introductory texts on justice and/or contemporary political philosophy. Unlike Adam Swift's *Political Philosophy: A Beginners' Guide for Students and Politicians*, it does not spend much time analysing concepts such as liberty and equality (Swift, 2006). Unlike Will Kymlicka's *Contemporary Political Philosophy* and Harry Brighouse's *Justice*, it does not conduct a detailed exploration of contemporary theories of justice (Brighouse, 2004; Kymlicka, 2001). Rather, it takes three of them – egalitarian liberalism, communitarianism, and libertarianism – as a framework within which to present debates on topical issues such as global justice and justice towards future generations. Unlike Jonathan Wolff's *An Introduction to Political Philosophy*, it does not say much about pre-twentieth-century philosophers (Wolff, 2006): in fact, Locke is the only major pre-twentieth-century thinker who appears in these pages. Like all four, however, it is unremittingly committed to presenting, as clearly and lucidly as possible, a wide range of arguments on some of the most pressing issues which face us today. Each in its own way has been an inspiration.

Above all, however, I want to express my gratitude to my students, who sat through badly timed lectures (at 2 p.m., immediately after lunch), commented on the accompanying handouts, politely tried not to yawn through yet another discussion of Rawls's original position, worried about the non-identity problem, enthusiastically endorsed Nozick's defence of private property in the second week of term only to reject it a month later, and insisted that a Briton is *not* entitled to give priority to the lives of his co-nationals (understandably so, perhaps, given the wonderfully international composition of the LSE's student body). Were it not for them, I would find my job rather boring. Thanks to them, it is an astoundingly privileged way of earning a living.

London, 2 February 2007

1 Setting the Stage

1 Introduction

One of the most important questions in contemporary political philosophy is that of which principles ought to regulate major social and political institutions, so as to ensure, as much as is feasible, that we are given what we are due. An answer to this question provides a theory of social justice: of social *justice*, in that it addresses the issue of what we owe to each other, and of *social* justice, in that it attends to the organization of societies. My aim, in this book, is not to provide such a theory. It is, rather, to describe some of the most important debates about social justice of the last thirty-five years – since, in fact, the publication of John Rawls's seminal *A Theory of Justice*. A theory of justice sets out *what* is owed to *whom*. In other words, it sets out the *content* of justice and delineates its *scope*. With respect to the question of scope, and until fairly recently, justice was seen, for the most part, as regulating what we owe to fellow, contemporary, citizens. On that view, then, justice requires, for example, that all citizens of the state be treated in the same way, regardless of their religion; or it requires that no citizen be allowed to live in poverty and destitution. Put differently, theories of justice sought to defend the territorially bounded and culturally homogeneous welfare state. As many commentators have argued, this is what *A Theory of Justice* does. In the last three decades or so, however, a number of challenges have been pressed against this rather simplistic (for some) understanding of justice. States are not culturally homogeneous: they are made up of many different ethnic and religious groups, who dispute the ideal of equality which underpins much of traditional thinking on justice, and some of whom want to set up their own state. Moreover, although they are, in some sense, territorially bounded, states are also subject to the growing pressures of an increasingly globalized world. They have to deal with transnational issues such as immigration and the distribution of resources across borders. In addition, greater awareness of the cost, for our successors, of our current economic and environmental policies has led some philosophers to argue that justice does not impose on us obligations merely to our contemporaries, but also to our successors (a point which Rawls in fact does address in *A Theory*). Finally, growing demands, on the part of the descendants of victims of injustice, for reparations (sometimes several hundred years later) question the view that only victims are owed compensation.

This book addresses these challenges to this understanding of the scope of justice, by examining the following six topics: justice between generations, justice between cultural groups, national self-determination and territorial justice, justice between foreigners, immigration, and reparations for past injustices. However, although the question of scope is analytically distinct from the question of content, one cannot secure a good grasp of the former without getting a sense of the latter. Merely to say, for example, that we have obligations of justice to distant strangers and not merely to fellow citizens, is misleading, as it might suggest that our obligations to the former are as weighty as our obligations to the latter. And yet, most people, both within and outside academia, believe that we owe more to fellow citizens than to foreigners, even though the scope of justice crosses national borders.

At this point, it is worth clarifying exactly what this book does, and how it does it. It does not articulate and defend a theory of its own: it is mainly descriptive and exploratory. Nor does it describe every single possible position on each of those topics. Nor does it present all the theories of justice which are currently being debated. It focuses on three such theories, namely egalitarian liberalism, communitarianism, and libertarianism. It does so, because those three theories each have something to say on the aforementioned issues. This calls for two comments. First, I do not mean to imply that other theories of justice are uninteresting or unimportant in their own right. Feminism, for example, is a rich and fascinating body of thought, which every student of political theory should familiarize herself, indeed *him*self, with. However, I will not treat it, here, as a distinct theory of justice alongside the aforementioned three schools of thought, simply because there does not seem to me to be a distinctively feminist position on, say, national self-determination or justice towards future generations. Instead, I will flag up feminist concerns on some of the topics at hand, as and when appropriate. (For a very good overview of gender in recent political theory, see Squires, 1999.)

Second, the treatment of our specific topics will on the whole lend itself well to a distinction between, say, communitarian and libertarian positions – in that there is, recognizably, a set of texts and arguments within those schools of thought on the issue at hand. Sometimes, however, one will not be able easily to apply those labels to a body of arguments on a particular issue. But one will be able to discern, in those arguments, some concerns raised by, respectively, egalitarian liberals, communitarians, and libertarians.

We will begin by setting out our three schools of thought. We will start with egalitarian liberalism (section 2), and in particular with Rawls's theory of justice (section 2.1). For it is with Rawls that the topic of social justice was given an enhanced profile in political philosophy. It is with Rawls too that perennial issues such as the relationship between individuals and communities and the distribution of resources from the affluent to the poor have returned to the fore of our discipline. Predictably, then, Rawls's theory is the basis for subsequent egalitarian liberal theories of justice, such as luck egalitarianism (section 2.2) and sufficientism (section 2.3). No less predictably, it is *against* Rawls that a number of philosophers have articulated and defended their own theories of social justice, most notably communitarians (section 3), and libertarians (section 4).

2 Egalitarian liberalism

A theory of justice is *liberal* in so far as it defends fundamental individual freedoms. It is *egalitarian* in so far as it assumes that all individuals are morally equal and mandates an extensive distribution of material resources (income and wealth) towards those who have fewer such resources. In contemporary political philosophy, egalitarian liberalism sprang from Rawls's major work, *A Theory of Justice*, which was first published in 1971 (Rawls, 1999a). Rawls's theory is rich and complex. Much attention has been focused on its distributive dimensions. In particular, egalitarian liberals disagree on the extent to which inequality matters. According to luck egalitarianism, inequality is intrinsically bad and individuals should not be made worse off through no fault of their own. According to sufficientism, inequality is not bad in and of itself, and all that matters is that individuals have enough resources.

2.1 Rawls's theory of justice

In *A Theory of Justice*, Rawls argues that a just society must distribute so-called primary goods, that is to say, the resources (income and wealth) and freedoms which all of us, as rational and moral agents, need to implement our conception of the good life. And it must do so according to two principles. The first principle, also known as the liberty principle, says that all individuals ought to enjoy basic liberties such as freedom of association and freedom of speech. The second principle states that inequalities in income and wealth are legitimate if, and only if, they benefit the worst-off members of society; in addition, such inequalities should attach to jobs and positions open to all.

Showing how we choose those principles of justice, and why we should choose them, is one of Rawls's main tasks in *A Theory*. As he puts it, we are very different from one another, we have different ideas as to how to lead our lives, have different talents and skills, and come from different backgrounds. Moreover, we are self-interested and thus primarily concerned with maximizing our own good. If we were to choose principles of justice in full knowledge of these facts, we would in fact choose principles which would systematically advantage us, at the expense of others. This would be wrong, for two reasons. First, we would obtain those advantages on the basis of social and natural contingencies (Rawls, 1999a, p. 17). For example, if we know that we are talented and thus have a high earning power, we will choose a tax system solely on the basis that it advantages us. But (according to Rawls) there is something deeply wrong about this. Take, for example, a supremely talented footballer who, in a Western country, is likely to earn millions of pounds a year. Why should he gain so much from something as arbitrary as the fact that he is lucky enough to be good with a football? After all, we are all moral equals, and such factors, which are traceable to pure luck, should not affect how we lead our lives.

Second, the most important thing about us is that we are autonomous agents. In other words, we have the capacity to frame, revise, and pursue a conception of the good life, and what matters to us is that we should be able to implement it. If we were to know what our conception of the good is, we would choose principles of justice by focusing on those rights and freedoms which are necessary to us, to the cost of rights and freedoms which are necessary to others. For example, if we know that we are, say, Catholic, we might be tempted to protect freedom of religion for Catholics only, unfairly overlooking the importance of their own religion for other groups.

Our task, then, is to ensure that primary goods are distributed in such a way as to nullify the impact of bad brute luck on our lives, and to enable us to implement whatever conception of the good we have.

In order to do so, we must put ourselves in a hypothetical situation and imagine how we would allocate primary goods if we did not know who we are, where we come from, in short, if we were behind a *veil of ignorance*. This contractual situation is called the *original position* and is a position of equality, since natural and social inequalities do not affect the principles of justice. In that sense, the principles we choose are the product of a *fair* agreement. That is why Rawls's theory is called *justice as fairness*.

In the original position, parties choose two principles. The liberty principle stipulates that each individual has a right to enjoy basic liberties, consistent with a similar and equal right for others. Rawls does not say much more than that, but we can surmise that he has in mind, apart from liberty of conscience, freedoms such as freedom of movement, private property, etc. – in short, the essential rights and freedoms of a liberal society.

So much, then, for the first principle of justice. The second principle comprises two parts: a principle for allocating material resources and a requirement that equal opportunities be secured to all. That is, social and economic inequalities are permitted provided that (a) they benefit the worst-off members of society, and (b) they attach to positions and offices open to all (Rawls, 1999a, p. 72). The first part of the second principle is also known as the difference principle, and the second part is known as the equal opportunity principle.

Note that the difference principle stipulates that income and wealth ought to be distributed equally, *unless* inequalities would benefit the worst-off members of society. This is quite a radical view, since it says, in effect, that equality is the default position – in other words, that it is inequality, and not equality, which stands in need of justification. However, Rawls believes that resources can be distributed unequally. This is because (according to him) talented people will not work to the full extent of their capacities if resources are distributed equally, with the effect that fewer resources will be available, through tax returns, for the worst off; but if the talented are rewarded more than the untalented while working at full capacity, then they will have an incentive to work to the full, and that will yield extra resources for the worst off. Suppose, for example, that I can work either as a doctor and earn a lot, or as a gardener and earn rather less. Suppose also that I would rather be a gardener. To distribute resources equally means imposing a 100 per cent rate of tax, and sharing the proceeds equally among all. Under that system, I get the same amount of income after tax no matter what I do, and so I have no incentive to take up medicine. Instead I will take up gardening and, as I will earn less than if I were a doctor, will contribute less to social wealth by way of taxes. As a result, there will be less wealth available for redistribution. If we distribute resources unequally, however, by imposing a lower rate of taxation, I may have to pay more tax as a doctor than I would as a gardener. But I would still get a higher income, and so I have an incentive to become a doctor. Since I will earn more than if I were a gardener, I will contribute more to social wealth by way of taxes, and there will be more wealth available for distribution. Clearly, the worst off, those who are in a position to earn less, will have more under an unequal distribution than under an equal distribution. Therefore, it would be rational for them to accept inequalities (Cohen, forthcoming).

To recapitulate briefly, then, Rawls argues that a just society is governed by the aforementioned two principles of justice, which are chosen by individuals themselves, in ignorance of their specific, individual characteristics such as their gender, race, and talents.

2.2 Egalitarian liberalism after Rawls, I: luck egalitarianism

Rawls's theory of justice is the bedrock, as it were, for one of the dominant theories of distributive justice, namely, luck egalitarianism. In academic and non-academic circles, the debate about equality is often framed as a debate between proponents of equality of opportunity, whereby you give people equal chances and leave it up to them to take those chances, and proponents of equality of outcomes, whereby you ensure that all end up with the same bundles of resources. Most egalitarians endorse equality of opportunity rather than equality of outcomes. Whether or not there is any space at all for equality of outcomes in a coherent theory of distributive justice remains a matter for debate (Phillips, 2004). In those stark terms, at any rate, luck egalitarianism does not seek to equalize outcomes. Its central position is not that individuals should have equal amounts of income, or resources, no matter how they came to be worse off than others. Rather, luck egalitarianism seeks to equalize opportunities. As a theory of equality of opportunity, however, it goes further than standard interpretations of that ideal. Not only does it clearly subscribe to the uncontroversial view that the law should not discriminate against individuals on the basis of arbitrary and unchosen factors such as gender and race. It also holds that inequalities arising from individuals' social and familial background should be remedied. However – and herein lies its claim to radicalism – it mandates the eradication of *all* inequalities which arise for reasons beyond individuals' control – including inequalities which arise from differences in *natural* talents and ability to command earning power.

At this juncture, we must draw two important distinctions which we will use throughout this section. First, we must distinguish between being made worse off as a result of the choices that we make, and being made worse off through bad luck. Suppose that I, unlike you, choose not to save any money at all, as a result of which, ten years later, I am worse off than you are. The inequality between us can be traced to choice. Suppose instead that I was born into a very poor family, whereas you were born into a rich one, as a result of which, in adulthood, I am worse off than you are. In this case, the inequality between us can be traced to luck.

Second, we must distinguish between bad *brute* luck and bad *option* luck. Suppose that we both choose to play the lottery. I end up losing a lot of money, whereas you end up winning. We both chose to run a similar risk of losing: I lost, you won, bad luck for me, good luck for you. But in so far as we both chose to play, the inequality between us can be traced to option luck. Contrast that case with the following: I become blind in an accident for which I am not responsible; you are fully sighted. The inequality between us can be traced to brute luck. Luck egalitarians believe that there is an important moral difference between those two inequalities. On their view, justice only requires the eradication of inequalities which are due to bad brute luck – not those which are due to bad option luck.

With this clarification out of the way, let us begin by revisiting Rawls's theory. According to Rawls, it would be unfair to choose principles for the allocation of primary goods on the basis of natural and social contingencies such as being very talented, being able-bodied, and coming from a privileged background: hence the original position and the veil of ignorance. Rawls insists, then, that primary goods in general, and income and wealth in particular, should be distributed in such a way as to neutralize the impact of bad brute luck on people's life: hence the two principles of justice, particularly the difference principle.

On closer inspection, however, and as Ronald Dworkin notes, the difference principle simply does not remedy inequalities due to bad brute luck (Dworkin, 1981a, 1981b). Consider the following case, involving two individuals of similar natural talents and background, who start off on an equal material footing. Peter decides to be a poet (which pays very little); Dan, by contrast, decides to become a doctor (which pays a lot). Predictably, Peter becomes worse off than Dan.

According to the difference principle, Peter should get as much from Dan as would be necessary to restore equality between them. Yet Peter is worse off than Dan because he *chose* an occupation which pays very little, even though he could have opted to become a doctor. The difference principle ends up subsidizing Peter's choice of the life of a poet. Why should Dan agree? It seems that the difference principle does not do what it aims to do, namely neutralize the impact of bad brute luck on people's life (Kymlicka, 2001).

Dworkin's aim, then, is to construct a theory of justice which does precisely that (Dworkin, 1981a, 1981b). According to Dworkin, all persons are owed equal concern and respect: we owe them equal *concern* if we ensure that they are not made worse off through no fault of their own. We owe them equal *respect* if we hold them responsible for the choices which they make, including bad choices. For that is what respecting people involves: it involves recognizing that they are moral and autonomous agents, that they have some degree of control over the way their life is going, and, accordingly, that they are responsible for many of the things – good or bad – which happen to them. A distributive principle which treats people with equal concern and respect allows inequalities consequent on bad option luck and bad choices, and disallows inequalities consequent on bad brute luck.

One of the important issues which Dworkin's theory addresses is that of the metric of equality: what is it, exactly, that should be equalized, if people are to be held responsible for their choices? Resources, welfare, opportunity for welfare, or access to advantage are some of the candidates (Dworkin, 1981a, 1981b; Arneson, 1989; Cohen, 1989). The literature on this issue is vast and complex, and I will not discuss it here in detail (see Kymlicka, 2001 for a very good discussion of it). Rather, I will focus on a key feature of luck egalitarianism, namely that individuals who are responsible for being worse off do not have a claim for help. More specifically, luck egalitarians say that people's expensive tastes ought not to be subsidized (Dworkin, 1981a). Suppose, for example, that you have a preference for photography as a hobby, whereas I have a preference for fishing. Photography is much more expensive than fishing; so, even if we have equal amounts of money, you will not be able to do as much photography as I can do fishing and will be worse off than me, at least in terms of preference satisfaction (Cohen, 1989, p. 923). In such a case I ought not to have to subsidize the costs of your expensive tastes, since you can, after all, choose to go fishing. We will return to the problem of expensive tastes later on in the book. For now, let me highlight some potential problems with the luck egalitarian view that people have a claim for help to the extent that they are not responsible for their predicament.

Consider, first, the problem of addictions. Suppose that someone is addicted to drugs or alcohol. And suppose moreover that he started consuming those products with only partial knowledge of what lay in store for him. Should he get treatment? His situation is different from that of someone who became addicted to crack while her mother, a crack addict herself, was expecting her. In the second case, luck egalitarians would recommend treatment, since the addict has no control over the origins of her addiction; in the first case, it is not clear what they would recommend (in the sense that they tend to avoid confronting the issue).

The difficulty posed by addictions points to a similar difficulty posed by so-called bad choices – choices which individuals make at one point in their life and which will cause them to be worse off than others at some later stages. Taken together, the problems of addictions and bad choices raise the issue of the role which individual responsibility should play in determining where individuals end up on the distributive scale. And at this juncture, the following two questions are worth asking. First, ought we really to hold individuals responsible for their bad choices, and thus ask them to pay for the costs of those choices, even if it means that they would end up living in severe destitution? Second, assuming that we ought to do just that, to what extent are individuals really responsible for their choices?

Let us turn to the first question. Throughout our lives we make decisions which may result in our becoming seriously needy. Does that mean that, as luck egalitarians would say, we lack a claim for compensation? This is not an impossibly abstract question. Consider the following cases. Someone cycles to work instead of taking easily available (and safer) public transport, and gets run over: should they be denied treatment if they cannot afford to pay for it privately? Someone has unprotected sex and becomes HIV positive: should they be denied retroviral drugs on the grounds that they should have known better? Someone decides to launch their own business, thereby taking considerable financial risks: should they be denied welfare benefits if the business goes bust? A woman takes time out of her job to look after her children or elderly relatives full-time: does this mean that, having not contributed the required number of years to a pension scheme, she should be left to live in poverty in old age?

As sufficientist critics such as Elizabeth Anderson have pointed out, the most radical versions of luck egalitarianism are extremely harsh towards individuals who make choices of these kinds (Anderson, 1999). We will assess their alternative proposals in section 2.3. Meanwhile, in response to the charge of harshness, some egalitarian philosophers distinguish between choices which it is reasonable for us to make in the course of our lives (cycling to work, taking time off from one's career to look after dependants, having sex with a condom and running the risk that the condom will rupture, etc.) and choices which it is not reasonable to make (skiing off beaten tracks, opting out of the job market to become a surfer, having unprotected sex, etc.). Misfortune attendant on the former kind of choices should be treated alongside misfortune for which individuals are not responsible; by contrast, misfortune arising from unreasonable choices does not warrant redress. Other egalitarians argue that we ought to hold individuals responsible for their choices until and unless the choices they make would leave them destitute. On that view, people's basic needs are met even if they are responsible for their predicament, but above that threshold, it is just that they should be asked to bear the costs of their choices (Clayton and Williams, 1999).

Is it, though? Luck egalitarians are committed to the view that the law should not be such as to prevent women from taking up a full-time job and in fact should disallow employers' discriminatory practices against women with respect to hiring, promotion, and remuneration. It seems, however, that they are also committed to the view that, if a woman chooses not to avail herself of the opportunity to earn what a full-time job would get her, and if she ends up worse off than men or than women who made a different choice, she would lack a claim for compensation. The problem, of course, is that gender-neutral laws in fact end up discriminating against women because the social pressures which lead women (and men) to avail themselves, or not, of the opportunities provided by those laws are more likely to operate to their detriment. In so far as women are socialized, in subtle and obvious ways, to see themselves as primary care-givers, one can doubt that they should be asked to bear the costs of their choice to become a carer, however autonomous that choice is (Mason, 2000, 2006).

This criticism of luck egalitarianism stems, in large part, from feminist worries about the oppression of women. As many feminists have pointed out, the pressures which lead women to make certain choices rather than others are felt most keenly in the family. And yet, what happens within the family is thought by many liberals to be largely beyond the reach of the law (bar the most severe cases of abuse), so that the liberal prescription that the public sphere should be kept separate from the private sphere is largely harmful to women (Pateman, 1989). Some egalitarian liberals have taken on board this particular strand of the feminist critique, and argued that justice is not merely about distributing, as it were, enforceable rights. Justice, they have claimed, also requires the fostering of an egalitarian social ethos, such that individuals are under obligations of justice to one another even if their failure to act in the required ways falls outside the remit of the law (Cohen, 2000). We will return to these points in chapters 2 and 3.

The feminist critique leads us straight to the second question raised by the problem of bad choices, namely that of the extent to which individuals *are* responsible for the choices they make. A first, obvious point is that we simply do not know. Take differences in earning power and income. We simply cannot assess the extent to which individuals are responsible for the fact that they are earning the amounts of money they do. The problem is not restricted to this particular issue. Remember the expensive taste problem. If I have been brought up on a grand family estate, surrounded by old master paintings, and if it has been drummed into me since childhood that this really is the only way to live my life, to what extent can I be said to carry responsibility for my expensive taste for such a lifestyle? And to the extent that I carry some responsibility for it, how can we trace it so as to distinguish what, in my choice, is mine, and what is not?

What lurks behind this criticism of the most radical versions of luck egalitarianism is the thought, which we encountered above, that individuals are not solely responsible for their choices – that the latter are in part informed by the social and familial milieu in which those individuals are born and raised. And it is for this reason that, according to some philosophers, we must look to inequalities between groups, and not solely between individuals, in order to get a handle on the extent to which the latter are unjust. To use an example given by John Roemer, we know, for instance, that middle-class white women are much less likely to smoke than working-class black men, and thus to suffer the ills attendant on regular smoking. Inequalities in health between those two types can thus reasonably be thought to be the product of their circumstances. On the other hand, inequalities in health between individuals *within* those types can thus reasonably be thought to be the product of their choices. An individual who is situated in the median of his type and is worse off than an individual who belongs to a type which does better along that particular dimension (say health) has a claim for compensation. By contrast, if he is situated below the median of his type, we can infer that he has made choices which others in his group did not make – choices, then, that were not dictated by his circumstances (Roemer, 1995, 1998; Anderson, 1999; Young, 2001).

There are some difficulties with such a view. In particular, if individuals ought not to be held responsible for their choices if those choices are broadly in line with what other members of their type choose, then it seems that they are responsible for rather little – too little, in fact, if one still wants to regard them as autonomous agents with some degree of control over their life (Phillips, 2006).

Luck egalitarians, then, face the following dilemma. Either they stick to their commitment to holding individuals responsible for their choices, in which case they are vulnerable to the aforementioned objections; or they seek to accommodate those objections by shrinking the range and kind of choices for which people really can be held responsible, and end up going too far in the other direction.

2.3 Egalitarian liberalism after Rawls, II: sufficientism

Sufficientists do not face that problem, because they do not believe that people ought to be denied help on the grounds that they are responsible for their predicament. Moreover, for sufficientists, what matters is not that individuals have as much as others (by way of resources, or welfare, or anything else, depending on your chosen metric), but that they have enough. Sufficientist theories reject equality as a distributive ideal, and in its place offer an account of what having enough means.

In drawing this distinction between luck egalitarians and sufficientists, I do not mean to suggest that the latter do not care about equality. Quite the contrary. For they too subscribe to what one may call the principle of fundamental equality, according to which all persons have equal moral worth and ought to be treated as such. In fact, it is worth noting that equality so understood matters to all (bar racist theories, obviously), even for libertarians of Nozick's ilk. As we shall see in section 4, for Nozick, treating people as equals means respecting their property rights over themselves and the product of their labour (even if this results in vast inequalities in wealth between the haves and the have nots: *these* inequalities, for libertarians, do not matter). Thus, disagreements between political philosophers centre not on the importance of treating people equally, but on what treating them equally means (Swift, 2006; see also Williams, 1973).

As I have just noted, sufficientists believe that treating people equally means ensuring that they have enough. By implication, they reject the view that inequalities matter in and of themselves. A full discussion of sufficientism would have to deal with both claims. In this section, however, I will only outline what 'having enough' means, since it is that particular issue, rather than the view that inequalities do not matter as such, which we will encounter in subsequent chapters (for sufficientist criticisms of the egalitarian view that inequalities matter as such, see Frankfurt, 1987; Raz, 1986; Crisp, 2006; for defences of the egalitarian view, see Arneson, 1993; Casal, 2007; Swift, 2006; Temkin, 1993).

According to Frankfurt, to have enough is to have the resources you need in order to implement your basic aims (Frankfurt, 1987). Others such as Anderson argue, more ambitiously, that to have enough means being able to function as a fully fledged member of one's society (Anderson, 1999). Others still borrow from Martha Nussbaum and Amartya Sen's work on capabilities. On this view, what matters is to ensure that individuals can live a life worthy of a human being. Such a life is one in which a number of central human functionings are present, such as being well nourished, being healthy, using one's senses, imagination and reason, having attachments to other people, and so on. What we owe each other, on that view, is to make sure that all of us are able to enjoy those functionings, in other words, that we all have the relevant capabilities (Nussbaum, 2000; Sen, 1992). Nussbaum and Sen are not sufficientists, in that they both (seem to) think that inequalities above a certain threshold do matter. However, the capabilities approach which they have defended, in both collaborative and separate works, has become very influential in sufficiency-based arguments about distributive justice, most notably – as we will see in chapter 5 – global distributive justice.

I will not review those various accounts of what having enough means in detail. Let me simply note some of the difficulties which their proponents need to tackle. Take the view that the sufficiency threshold should be defined by reference to needs, for example. Above and beyond basic needs, it is actually quite difficult to establish what is a need, and what is merely a want, or a preference (see, e.g., Miller, 1999a; Wiggins, 1986). Or take Frankfurt's account, whereby to have enough means having the resources necessary to implement one's basic aims, provided those aims are reasonable. According to him, once someone has those resources, she has no reason to want more, and that is when we can say that she has enough. The problem, of course, is that it may in fact be reasonable for someone always to want more: why should there be an upper limit to reasonableness? In addition – and this is a more serious problem – on that definition of sufficiency, there is no reason to help the very poor or the poor, rather than the well off. For the latter may well have reasonable aims which they cannot implement without extra help. Assuming that they need as much as, or less than, the poor or the very poor need to implement *their* own basic aims, why should we help the very poor, rather than the well off (Arneson, 1993)?

Anderson's account of the meaning of having enough avoids those particular problems. For her, having enough means having the resources necessary to function as a full citizen in a social democracy. However, above and beyond basic needs, it is very hard to decide what people need in order to function as a full citizen in a social democracy. Set the sufficiency threshold too low, and individuals will not get what they need in order fully to function. Set it too high, and it will be vulnerable to the charge that, above and beyond basic needs, it is impossible to assess objectively what having enough means. In fact, any such attempt will smack of cultural bias and lack of sensitivity to individuals' own understanding of what they need – a charge, incidentally, which has also been levelled against the capabilities approach.

To conclude, sufficientist theories differ from luck egalitarianism in some important ways. However, they too subscribe to the principle of fundamental equality. Moreover, neither luck egalitarians nor sufficientists are wedded to the view that distributive justice is the only value that matters. Thus, the former may accept that, under conditions of extreme scarcity, one ought to ensure that as many people as possible live, rather than die, even if this mandates an inegalitarian distribution of resources. Likewise, a sufficientist whose account of the meaning of having enough is particularly demanding may well concede that, in the face of the sacrifices which obligations of justice would impose on those who have more than enough, justice ought to give way. To repeat, justice is not the only thing that matters: in particular, our relationships with others, such as our friends and family, matter too; so do our own goals and projects. And it might be that we simply cannot be required to sacrifice them for the sake of eradicating unchosen disadvantage or ensuring that all have enough (Nagel, 1989). Deciding where to draw the line is beyond the scope of this book. Suffice it to say that we will encounter this tension between justice and other values when discussing the issues of global distributive justice and immigration.

3 The communitarian critique of Rawls: individuals and communities

So much, then, for egalitarian liberalism. In this section, we review an enduring and important critique of it, namely communitarianism. There are many strands within communitarianism, which we will not review in full here. (For superb accounts of the debate between liberals and communitarians, see Buchanan, 1989; Mulhall and Swift, 1996.) Instead, we will focus on some of the criticisms which major communitarian thinkers such as Alasdair McIntyre, Michael Sandel, Charles Taylor and Michael Walzer deploy in the works which they published in the decade or so following the publication of *A Theory of Justice* (McIntyre, 1981; Sandel, 1996; Taylor, 1979a, 1986; Walzer, 1983). Communitarians target their criticisms at Rawls specifically. However, as will be clear throughout this book, in many ways their arguments apply to egalitarian liberalism in general. In this section, we will focus on three of their objections against Rawls: (1) his understanding of the ways in which we should conceive of justice is misguided; (2) his account of the relationship between individual and community is unsound; (3) his theory attaches far too much importance to individual rights. Not all of those communitarian thinkers make all three criticisms in the terms just described. All of them, however, one way or another take the Rawls of 1971 – and his egalitarian liberal successors – to task for mistakenly grounding justice on universal foundations, and for overlooking the (non-instrumental) importance of communal values.

3.1 Thinking about justice

In *A Theory of Justice*, Rawls claims that the principles of justice apply universally, to all individuals irrespective of their culture. Communitarians take issue with this view, on two (independently argued) grounds. Thus, for Sandel, to conceive of justice as a set of principles chosen by individuals who do not know anything about themselves is to appeal to a faulty conception of the self – a self prior to its ends, a self which can be apprehended without understanding of its ends. According to Sandel, this is problematic for several reasons. For a start, that is not how we perceive ourselves. We do not see ourselves as disembodied but, rather, as people who are located in time and space, as well as in a network of deep relationships which are important to us. In addition, and contrary to what Rawls suggests, we *identify* with our ends: they are part of who we are, which they would not be if we were entirely prior to them. Moreover, it is not only that the self is constituted by its ends; it is also that, in fact, it does not *choose* its ends. In other words, Rawls's voluntaristic conception of the self is flawed.

If Sandel is correct, then it does not make sense, indeed, to derive conclusions about what justice requires of us by appealing to the choices which disembodied selves would make behind a veil of ignorance. Nor does it make sense to conceive of justice as universal in scope: for in so far as the individual is constituted by his ends, and in so far as (as we will see below) those ends are shaped by the social environment in which individuals live, justice itself is in fact dependent on such an environment. Interestingly, some feminists are sympathetic to Sandel's criticism of Rawls. They too claim that it is profoundly misguided to conceive of individuals as disembodied, separate from others and able to distance themselves from their social and familial responsibilities. More fundamentally, it is a mistake to think of individuals as able to reason in abstraction from the context and practices within which reason is exercised. In so far as gender plays a crucial role in shaping those contexts and practices in such a way as to ensue in the subordination of women, any theory of justice which affirms that gender is irrelevant and that reason is abstract will fail to give women proper respect (Jaggar, 1983). In that regard, this particular feminist critique of Rawls is sympathetic to communitarian concerns about the necessity to contextualize norms and the reasoning process by which they are derived.

Michael Walzer reaches a somewhat similar conclusion, via a different route. According to Walzer, a just society is not one which treats its members according to some universal principles: 'a given society is just if its substantive life is lived in a certain way – that is, in a way faithful to the shared understanding of its members . . . Justice is rooted in the distinct understandings of places, honors, jobs, things of all sorts, that constitute a shared way of life. To override those understandings is (always) to act unjustly' (Walzer, 1983, pp. 313–14).

Walzer's conception of justice is particularistic because it is tied to the particular understandings of jobs, goods, etc., of the individual members of a given society. And the reason, in turn, why Walzer thinks that justice is particularistic is this: we are one another's equal, and in particular are producers of social meanings. To respect one another as equal producers of such meanings is to show respect for other people's opinions, and not to impose on them a conception of how they should live with which they do not identify. For example, Walzer notes that Athenians in the fifth and fourth centuries BC used public funds to subsidize gymnasiums and public baths, not to help the very needy (1983, p. 67). Who are *we* to say that the Athenians were wrong? On what grounds do we deem ourselves justified in imposing on them values which they reject? After all, we ourselves, as members of liberal societies, believe that all human beings are worthy of equal respect. We should therefore live by that principle when approaching different cultures. Importantly for arguments about multiculturalism and global distributive justice which we will examine later on, if Walzer is right, then it is hard to see how one can conceive of justice as applying across borders and across cultural groups, since different groups have different conceptions of how they want to allocate their resources. As some feminists have argued, however, Walzerian accounts of justice face the following difficulty. In order to say that a given society has a given set of *shared* understandings, we must be able to identify *whose* understandings they are, and, in turn, to identify the processes by which they are articulated. Once we do that, however, we come to realize that those supposedly shared understandings are usually shaped and articulated by privileged groups – the dominant race or ethnic group in societies organized along racial lines, and the dominant gender – men – in most societies (Okin, 1989).

3.2 Individuals and communities

Not only, then, are Rawlsian liberals misguided (as far as communitarians are concerned) in their meta-understanding of justice; they articulate a problematic view of the relationship between individuals and communities. Thus, according to both Sandel and McIntyre, the voluntaristic conception of the self cannot make sense of many familiar phenomena of moral life. For example, it cannot make sense of the fact that we can deeply identify with a political cause or a particular relationship, and that we can feel shaken *to the core* when that political cause or relationship fails. What we feel, in those cases, is not simply that we have not achieved our ends or met our goals. Rather, we feel that *we* have failed. Similarly, the liberal conception of the self does not make sense of what happens when we feel torn apart by different commitments to our family, to our friends, and to our country. For if we could simply choose those commitments, we would be able to choose, relatively painlessly, which are the most important: we would not feel *torn apart*. And yet we do feel that way. In a nutshell, communal attachments are integral to the person, in ways which Rawlsian liberals fail to recognize (Sandel, 1996, esp. ch. 1; McIntyre, 1981, esp. chs. 3 and 15; Taylor, 1979a, pp. 157ff.).

This general critical point on the Rawlsian conception of the relationship between individuals and their communities is developed by Sandel, McIntyre, and Taylor along the following three lines. First the liberal individual is self-interested and self-seeking, and regards communal attachment, in a purely instrumental way, as what furthers his own interests. According to communitarians, society so understood is very different from many other, richer, fuller conceptions of the communal life, which it is within the remit of the state to promote and protect.

Second, the liberal individual does not accept obligations which he has not voluntarily placed on himself. Such is the gist of the social contract tradition, in which we are bound to obey a rule to the extent that we consent to it. And yet, communitarians would press, individuals are under obligations to which they have not consented, and which they acquire simply in virtue of their membership in a group. Take familial obligations, for example. We incur obligations to our parents (for example, to look after them in their old age) not because we choose to incur them, but because we belong, with our parents, to a family unit. Likewise, membership in a wider community, such as the nation, also imposes on individuals obligations of that kind.

Third, the liberal individual retreats into the private sphere, and is not thought to attach importance to communal, and political, ways of life. Thus, the liberal individual is not in any way obliged to take interest in the political and social matters of the community. Again, according to communitarians, particularly Sandel and McIntyre, this is a very impoverished conception of the relationship that ties the individual to his or her community.

3.3 Justice and rights

The third important strand of the communitarian critique of Rawlsian liberalism pertains to the importance which the latter attaches to individual rights, and particularly to the idea of universal human rights. While Rawls does not systematically couch his theory of justice in the language of rights (thus, the difference principle is not rights-based), it is undeniable that liberals on the whole do so. In fact, one could go as far as to say that justice, in contemporary liberalism, is about assigning rights. To put the point differently, in contemporary liberalism, it is not enough to say that individuals generally have an obligation to respect others' freedoms and provide them with the required resources. More strongly, they have an obligation *to* one another to do so, which is another way of saying that they all have rights against one another to do so. Those rights, moreover, are enforceable; that is to say, they are moral rights which the state ought to recognize as legal rights.

Here, we must distinguish between two variants of the communitarian critique of the primacy of rights and of the legalist, and divisive, ethos which they promote. On the one hand, some communitarians such as McIntyre dispute that there are such things as rights in the first instance: rights, on their view, are nothing but chimera, for which no rational, grounded argument exists (McIntyre, 1981, ch. 1).

On the other hand, some communitarians, such as Sandel, agree that individuals do have rights, but deny that those rights override communal views in the ways, and to the extent, that Rawlsian liberals say that they do. More strongly, for Sandel, rights fail to promote community values. Consider the right to freedom of speech. If it is given the kind of protection which it enjoys in, say, the United States, it violates important community values such as repugnance about pornography. For anyone involved in the pornography industry can then oppose any attempt to curb pornography on the grounds that such attempts constitute violations of the right to freedom of speech. But what if we, as a community, wish to protect our children from pornographic material? What if we, as a community, believe that pornography degrades women and should be censored? Why should we not do so? Why should the individual right to publish and express whatever one wants be given such priority (Sandel, 1984)?

More strongly still, rights, and justice in general, can be seen only as a remedy to social conflicts, not as the primary expression of our commitment to one another as members of the same community. For if we were united as a community, and if we had a shared understanding of the values we want to pursue and the ways we want to treat each other, rights and justice would not be necessary. The core question, then, is how to develop those understandings, not how to deal with the fact that we do not have them.

3.4 Rawls's response: political liberalism

In 1993, Rawls published his second major book, *Political Liberalism*, in which he clarifies a number of the claims he made in *A Theory of Justice*, partly in response to the communitarian critique (Rawls, 1993). In the remainder of this book, when I refer to Rawls, I will be referring to the author of *A Theory*. Still, his reply to communitarians is worth mentioning here, for the record. First, his conception of justice, he claims, is *political*, and not comprehensive. That is, it rests on a political conception of the person and applies to the basic political and social institutions of society, and not to all its institutions. In saying that his conception of the person is political, Rawls is affirming, explicitly, that persons, on his view, are capable of detaching, and ought to detach, themselves from their ends and attachments when thinking about principles of justice. He is not supposing that they are capable of detaching, and ought to detach, themselves from their ends, in their everyday lives, as parents, churchgoers, workers, members of associations, etc. This is why he also believes that his conception of the person, political as it is, is compatible with a variety of comprehensive, metaphysical doctrines about what persons actually are.

Relatedly, Rawls is quite clear that his principles of justice apply to the basic structure, that is, to society's major political and social institutions. For him, then, the scope of justice is limited, and individuals, in their private lives as parents, churchgoers, association members, etc., can deploy, and pursue, a variety of comprehensive, moral conceptions of what the good life is.

Moreover, far from being actually universal, his theory, Rawls claims, makes sense of the fundamental and shared ideals constitutive of a democratic society. Here, then, he echoes Walzer's claim that a theory of justice should be sensitive to the social and shared understandings of a given community at a given time. Whether, on Rawls's view, it is desirable that all societies should become democratic is another question.

Finally, far from being insensitive to the importance of communal goods, his theory of justice, he claims, is clearly one in which citizens attach importance to the value of political participation, and unite, as citizens, around the shared communal goals of realizing justice.

Thus, Rawls, in *Political Liberalism*, seems to qualify *A Theory of Justice* in important ways. And the reason, in turn, why that is so is what he calls the fact of reasonable pluralism. In democratic and diverse societies, he notes, individuals will hold different comprehensive moral and metaphysical doctrines. Respect for individuals requires, therefore, that we come up with a theory of justice which does not presuppose the truth of any such doctrine. This conception is *political* in that individuals, as rational and moral *citizens*, can all endorse it, regardless of their own comprehensive moral doctrines. More precisely, this requires that, when we try to justify to one another why we should adopt a given principle of justice rather than another, we must deploy in support of our conclusion reasons which all can endorse. Those reasons, which Rawls calls *public* reasons, must thus be unhinged from comprehensive moral, metaphysical, and religious doctrines.

What can communitarians make of this response? They will find Rawls's departure from his initial universalistic aspirations congenial to their own theories. However, they are likely to remain unconvinced by his insistence that his theory of justice is truly political, rather than comprehensive. For a start, they (and some other liberals) might want to say that, in areas such as abortion and bioethics in general, we must know what a person is before we can decide, for example, whether the foetus qualifies as a person, and thus whether abortion is morally permissible and should remain legal. In so far as such decisions pertain to what the law should say, they apply to the basic structure, and are within the scope of a theory of justice. Theories of justice, thus, cannot hope to avoid making metaphysical assumptions about what persons are.

Relatedly, Rawls's account of justice as deployed in *Political Liberalism* draws a sharp distinction between the personal and the political domains. In the political domain, he argues, we ought to detach ourselves from our ends; but we need not do so in the personal domain. Communitarians are likely to doubt that we can behave so differently depending on which domain we operate in.

4 The libertarian critique of Rawls: justice as entitlements

The communitarian critique of Rawlsian justice focuses on his account of how we should conceive of justice, and of the relationship between individuals and communities. By contrast, the libertarian critique, which we examine in this section, focuses on Rawls's claim that individuals are under an obligation of justice to distribute material resources in such a way as to improve the situation of the worst off. According to libertarians, coercive taxation for such purposes is illegitimate, because it undermines individual freedom.

There are a number of libertarian thinkers, whose works we cannot assess here in detail. Instead, we will focus on Robert Nozick's important *Anarchy, State and Utopia*, in which we find the most sophisticated critique of Rawlsian justice to come from this particular school of thought, and whose theory of justice has its root in the political thought of John Locke (Nozick, 1974). Here again, although Nozick focuses on Rawls, his critique of *A Theory* does apply to egalitarian liberalism in general.

According to Nozick, a theory of distributive justice is comprised of three principles. First, there is a principle of acquisition, which sets out the conditions under which individuals come to legitimately own resources which are not owned by anyone yet. Second, there is a principle of transfer, which sets out the conditions under which individuals come to legitimately transfer their ownership rights to other parties. Third, there is a principle of compensation, which sets out what compensation is owed by those who violate the principles of acquisition and transfer. Rawls's difference principle, Nozick argues, ought to be rejected. It appears reasonable only because the goods to be distributed are considered to be manna from heaven, that is, resources to which no one has prior entitlements. However, those goods, Nozick claims, in fact, are produced by the talented, through their work, and one must take this into account. And by working on things, Nozick insists, we acquire ownership rights over them. Thus, the difference principle, and by implication coercive taxation for distributive purposes, violates individuals' ownership rights over the product of their labour and, thereby, over themselves.

In order, then, to understand Nozick's theory of justice, we must get to grips with his account of acquisition. At its heart, we find the notion of self-ownership, whereby we have full rights of ownership over ourselves – just as we have over things. More precisely, this means that we, and only we, have the right to decide how our body, talents, and productive capacities will be used. Through the deployment of those capacities we produce things, and derive wealth from them. In that sense, coercive taxation is not merely an interference with our property rights in things, it is also an interference with our property rights over *ourselves*. We will examine the connection between ownership of ourselves and ownership of things in a moment. For now, let us look at the notion of self-ownership.

The first thing to note is that self-ownership is a matter of rights: just as individuals have rights in things, they have rights over their bodies and persons. Those rights are negative rights, in that they impose on others a duty not to interfere with their holders (whereas positive rights, such as the right to food, impose duties on others to do something for the sake of their holders). Moreover, self-ownership rights are natural rights, in that they are held by all human beings, in virtue of the fact that they are human beings. Nozick's claim is not new, but echoes John Locke's view, which he articulates in his *Second Treatise of Government*, that all human beings own themselves, in virtue of being human. Finally, rights are side-constraints on other people's actions. That is, to have a right means that others are not allowed to act in certain ways.

The self-ownership thesis – that is, the thesis that we enjoy rights of ownership over ourselves – yields two claims. First, individuals ought not to have to live under social and political arrangements to which they have not consented: for to coerce them to do certain things, or not to do them, would violate their rights over themselves. In short, individual consent is a necessary condition for the legitimacy of political and social institutions. Second, coercive taxation for purposes other than maintaining the most minimal of states is unjust. This is because coercive taxation compels A, who rightfully owns the resources at his disposal, to transfer part of his resources to B: in so doing, it violates A's freedom.

Now, in order to assess whether Nozick is right, we need to know how to move from self-ownership to ownership of material resources. That is, we need to know how one gets from the view that we own ourselves to the view that we have private rights of ownership over the world, such that coercive taxation for the purpose of helping others is illegitimate.

At this point, we should be able to discern, in *Anarchy, State and Utopia*, a coherent account of the principle of acquisition – of the principle in virtue of which the fact that I own myself enables me to acquire ownership rights over material resources. Interestingly, however, Nozick does not set out his principle of acquisition in any kind of detail. Instead, he reviews Locke's theory of acquisition, which occupies a central place in section 5 of the *Second Treatise of Government*. In fact, one can distinguish five different arguments, in Locke, for the right to own property. The most famous and often discussed – and on which Nozick focuses – goes like this (1974, pp. 174ff.).

1 Man owns himself, i.e., owns his person and his labour.
2 When he labours on nature (e.g., catches a fish, picks up an apple), man mixes his labour, which belongs to him, with that thing.
3 If you take away the resulting product from man without man's consent, you are taking away, with it, his labour.
4 In doing so, you are violating his ownership right over his labour. Therefore,
5 The resulting product must be his (it is the only way to respect his ownership right over his labour).

This particular argument for private property has a lot of intuitive appeal. Imagine that you are taking a walk in the country, and that there is an apple tree there which you know does not belong to anyone.

You pick up an apple and are about to eat it when someone snatches it away from you: many of you would probably say 'Hey, hang on! I have just picked it up, it's mine!' Or imagine that you are ploughing a piece of land which has not been claimed, yet, by anyone else, and that someone takes a sizeable portion of the harvest without your permission. Here again, you would probably protest, on the grounds that, as *you* worked on that land, the harvest is all yours. It seems that this is what Locke had in mind. But when one looks at his argument more closely, one can see that it is hugely problematic, as Nozick himself admits. For a start, neither action nor task is the sort of thing that can be mixed with an object. And even if it makes sense to say that we own our labour and that we mix it with objects and resources, it is unclear that we retain an entitlement to our labour once it is mixed: for once it is mixed, our labour disappears into the object and ceases to exist as such. As Nozick himself puts it, if I spill a can of tomato juice into the sea, do I lose my can, or do I acquire the whole of the sea (1974, p. 175)?

Finally, as Nozick asks: 'What are the boundaries of what labor is mixed with?' (1974, p. 174). If I put a fence around a plot of land, or a flag atop a mountain, do I own the bit of land which is immediately underneath the fence, or that which is enclosed? Do I own the top of the mountain, or the whole of it? Locke does not settle those issues. Nor does Nozick, and yet they are crucially important. Any theory of acquisition, and in particular of acquisition of territories, which invokes principles such as labour, or first occupancy along the lines 'I laboured on *that*, so *that* belongs to me', or 'I got *there* first, so that belongs to me', will have to delineate what *that* and *there* exactly mean. As we will see in chapter 4, the conflict between Israelis and Palestinians is, in part, a conflict between two peoples who invoke first occupancy and labour in support of their claim that they should enjoy sovereignty over part or the whole of Israel.

Nozick himself, then, is not convinced by Locke's theory of acquisition, or at least by one of its principles (the mixing labour principle). However, in so far as he subscribes to the self-ownership thesis, he endorses the first step in that principle, namely, (1) man owns himself, i.e., owns his person and his labour. And he does seem to think that taking away the product of man's labour without his consent amounts to taking away his labour, which in turn violates his rights of self-ownership and thereby undermines his freedom. While he does not provide an argument for this view, he nevertheless sets a limit on appropriation. Working on things, he claims, is not enough to ground property rights in them. One must also make sure that one does not worsen other people's situation by doing so. Again, this is an idea which he derives from Locke. For Locke too imposes a proviso on appropriation – the so-called Lockean proviso – whereby we can acquire property legitimately only if we leave 'enough, and as good left in common for others' (Locke, 1988).

Nozick notes that there is a weak and a strong form of the proviso. On the strong version, one stipulates that appropriation is legitimate if, and only if, it does not worsen other people's opportunities to appropriate things. On the weak form, one stipulates that appropriation is legitimate if, and only if, it does not worsen other people's opportunities to *use* things. As Nozick notes, the strong proviso is problematic in the following way (1974, p. 176). Imagine someone, Z, who is not left with enough to appropriate; if so, Y, who appropriated before him, did so illegitimately. This means that Y was left worse off by his predecessor, X, than he would have been if Z had not been around to appropriate resources. But if Y himself was left worse off by X, then X appropriated illegitimately, and so on. By going backwards all the way to A, one can see that A himself could not have appropriated legitimately. If we go for the strong version of the Lockean proviso, it seems that appropriation can never be legitimate.

According to Nozick, then, the weak proviso is preferable. In fact, he argues that it offers people new opportunities which they did not have before other people's appropriation. Generally, private property as an institution has much in its favour: it enables us to use resources efficiently, to better experiment in business, science, etc. Finally it allows for the creation of other, better resources (Nozick, 1974, p. 177). I will not discuss the proviso in detail. One of its features is worth mentioning, though. As G. A. Cohen points out, its operation requires that we compare two states of affairs, S1, where agent A appropriates resources R and leaves B in a given situation (better off, worse off, or equally well off), and a counterfactual state of affairs, S2, where A does not appropriate R and leaves B in a given situation. As Cohen notes, the proviso as defended by Nozick supposes that the relevant counterfactual is one where R would have to be left unowned. However, there is no reason to exclude other counterfactuals where B himself appropriates R (Cohen, 1995). We will return to the importance of using the right counterfactuals, in this kind of reasoning, in chapter 7.

Interestingly, Nozick acknowledges that some appropriations will make other people worse off in that they will not even be able to *use* resources: imagine that I buy all available supplies of the same essential goods and that, by some catastrophe, everybody else's supplies are wiped out. Given that those goods are both necessary for survival and scarce, I have made other people worse off by appropriating everything, and I thus act wrongly.

In sum, there are limits to what we can appropriate. Nozick does not spell out what this entails, in principle. But some philosophers have argued that this may well justify coercive taxation for the purpose of ensuring that those who are made worse off in violation of the Lockean proviso get compensation (Kymlicka, 2001). In fact, Nozick himself seems to agree (Nozick, 1974, pp. 230–1). Thus, whereas the principles of acquisition and transfer do, on the face of it, seem to rule out coercive taxation, the principle of compensation does, on the face of it, seem to allow for it. We will come back to this issue in chapter 7, when we address in greater detail the issue of compensation for historical injustice.

5 Themes and issues

In sections 2 to 4, I set out egalitarian liberalism, communitarianism, and libertarianism. My aim, in those sections, was not to offer a detailed analysis of those views. Rather, it was to set the background against which we will review some of the main current disputes about justice. Accordingly, it pays to remind ourselves, at this stage, of the questions and issues which we have raised so far and which we will encounter at various points in the remainder of this book.

First, then, the principles of justice, in *A Theory of Justice*, are meant to apply at all times and in all places. As we saw, communitarians and some feminists dispute this, on the grounds that the context within which those obligations arise actually does matter. We will revisit this when looking at multiculturalism and global justice in chapters 3 and 5 respectively.

Second, a just society, according to Rawls, is one which transfers resources from the better off to the worse off, so as to bring about equality in the distribution of primary goods, unless an unequal distribution would benefit the worse off. Libertarians of Nozick's ilk take issue with coercive taxation, and deploy an account of justice whereby individuals own themselves. From the thesis of self-ownership are derived two principles, the principle that they own the resources which they produce, and the principle that they ought not to be subject to principles to which they have not consented. As we will see in chapters 3 to 6, arguments about multiculturalism, national self-determination, territorial justice, global justice, and immigration often invoke some form of those two principles in defence of the view that individuals have the right to form national communities and that, once they have done so, they have the right to withhold social wealth from, and bar access to, non-members.

Third, assuming, against libertarians, that coercive taxation is legitimate, several questions still arise. In particular, are individuals under an obligation to provide assistance to distant strangers in time (future generations) or in space (foreigners), and, if so, assistance of what kind? We will deal with these issues in chapters 2, 5, and 6.

2 Justice towards Future Generations

1 Introduction

As I noted in chapter 1, traditional accounts of justice hold that we have obligations of justice towards fellow citizens who are our contemporaries. In this chapter, we examine a first challenge to this standard view on the scope of justice, whereby we have obligations to future generations. As we will see, extending the scope of justice over time will have implications for the question of the content of our obligations.

Clearly, the question of justice towards future generations has generated considerable debate in recent years, particularly on climate change, the consumption of non-renewable natural resources, and energy policy. Before outlining the various positions which egalitarian liberals, communitarians, and libertarians take on the issue of justice towards future generations, a number of clarificatory points are in order. First, in asking what a given generation owes to its successors, I will ask what *a birth cohort* owes to succeeding birth cohorts, rather than what *an age group* owes to other age groups. A cohort is a class of individuals who experience a particular event – birth, marriage, graduation, etc. – at the same time. Thus, all individuals born in 2006 belong to the same birth cohort. An age group is a class of individuals who are of the same age, but do not necessarily coexist. Thus, individuals aged forty in 1688 belong to the same age group as individuals aged forty in 1789. Whether justice between future generations is seen as justice between birth cohorts or between age groups matters crucially. In the first case, one looks at what a given generation is under an obligation to do for the sake of its successors. For example, one decides whether a given generation must leave the environment in as good a shape as it has found it. In the second case, one looks at what, at a specific point in time, say in 2006, a given age group, say those aged fifty, must do for the sake of some other age group, say those aged twenty. For example, one decides whether it is appropriate for the former to raise the compulsory age of retirement (which would be in their interest), thereby increasing competition for jobs and making it harder for twenty-year-olds to access the job market. And that, one might think, is unjust. In this chapter, though, we will focus on justice between birth cohorts.

Second, we need to be aware that a claim of the form 'G_2 owes x to G_3' admits of two interpretations, namely (a) 'individual members of G_2 owe x to individual members of G_3' or (b) 'G_2 as a group owes x to G_3 as a group'. As we shall see, theories of justice which take as their starting point the claim that individuals, and not groups, are the fundamental moral units seem to be committed to (a), which in turn raises a number of serious difficulties.

Third, the words 'future generations' need disambiguating. Imagine that we have three generations: G_1, G_2, G_3. G_3 does not exist yet; G_1 and G_2 overlap. From the point of view of G_1, the question of justice between generations (by which, to reiterate, I will mean birth cohorts) must be divided into two sub-questions: whether G_1 owes anything to G_3 – in other words, to future people – and if so, what; whether G_1 owes anything to G_2, and if so, what. Quite obviously, it is easier to justify obligations to overlapping generations, for example on grounds of reciprocity. On the reciprocity view, G_1 has obligations to G_2, with which it overlaps, because it will receive benefits from G_2 once its members are full contributors to society's wealth. As we will see, however, a number of philosophers have sought to justify obligations to distant, non-overlapping generations.

Fourth, one must distinguish between three different kinds of policies which G_1 will typically conduct vis-à-vis its successors:

Savings: G_1 passes on to its successors more wealth and opportunities than it has itself enjoyed.

Dis-savings: G_1 passes on to its successors less wealth and fewer opportunities than it has itself enjoyed.

Status quo: G_1 passes on to its successors exactly what it has itself enjoyed.

Thus, one may hold one of the four following views:

1 G_1 does exactly as it wishes: savings, dis-savings, and status quo are all allowed.
2 G_1 must save, which implies that dis-savings and status quo are prohibited.

3 G_1 can save (but does not have to do so, which allows status quo),
   and must not dis-save.
4 G_1 can neither save nor dis-save, in other words, the status quo is
   mandatory.

Fifth, there are different ways in which G_1 can pass on more, or
fewer, opportunities and more, or less, wealth to its successors. For
example, it is sometimes argued that environmental pollution for
which we are currently responsible thins the ozone layer, with disas-
trous consequences for the environment (such as increased tempera-
tures, melting of the northern and southern ice caps, advancing
deserts and erosion of coastlines, hence less and less habitable land,
etc.). Consider, too, highly consumerist policies which deplete the
total capital available to our successors, by imposing on them high
levels of collective debts which they will have to service. Consider,
finally, policies of unfettered population growth, which result in fewer
resources per capita three or four generations down the line. In other
words, we affect our successors by making decisions relative to the
kind of environment in which they will live, to the amount of wealth
which they will have at their disposal, and to the size of the generation
to which they will belong.

This fifth point calls for a few additional remarks. For a start,
whether or not we save or dis-save is a factor of all three kinds of policy
(environmental policy, economic policy, or population policy). Thus,
we dis-save if we pass on less wealth to our successors than we have
received, even though the size of their population is the same as ours.
We also dis-save if we pass on *more* wealth to them than we have
received *and* if the size of their population is greater than ours.
Throughout this chapter, we will refer to all three kinds of policies.

Moreover, when talking about the environment, one must bear in
mind that environmental goods can be part of a theory of justice in at
least two ways. On the one hand, they can be seen as the precondition
for enjoying other goods (so that, for example, an unpolluted environment provides the conditions under which human beings can enjoy
the good of health). On the other hand, they can also be regarded as a
set of goods to be enjoyed in and of themselves (such as an area very
rich in wildlife and great natural beauty). In addition, one must attend
to different ways in which we save, or dis-save, with respect to the
environment. Thus, we dis-save if we pollute the environment, since
our successors will function under less favourable conditions than we
have had, and will enjoy fewer environmental goods than we did. We

also dis-save if we appropriate finite, non-renewable natural resources without providing our successors with alternatives. I will not, within the scope of this chapter, attend to those various aspects of the issue of justice and the environment in any detail. Rather, I will merely allude to them as and when appropriate.

Finally, on some views, the environment has moral status in and of itself, and warrants protecting for its own sake. Less controversially, others argue that our obligations with respect to the environment comprise obligations to attend to the welfare of non-human animals, for animals' sake rather than ours. Again, space prevents me from addressing those various questions here. Rather, I shall focus on anthropocentric accounts of our obligations with respect to the environment.

Those clarificatory points give us some sense of the sheer complexity of the issue of justice towards future generations. In what follows, I will sketch out some of the ways in which some egalitarian liberals (section 2), some communitarians (section 3), and some libertarians (section 4) have dealt with it. I will then outline an important objection to the idea of obligations to future generations (section 5).

2 Egalitarian liberalism and future generations

As was clear in chapter 1, luck egalitarians and sufficientists argue that individuals are under an obligation to help their contemporaries – indeed, that the latter have a right to receive such help. In this section, we examine Rawls's stand on our obligations to our successors, leaving our discussion of the luck egalitarian and sufficientist positions until sections 2.2 and 2.3 respectively.

2.1 Rawls's just savings principle
Rawls's position on justice towards future generations is to be found in §44 of *A Theory of Justice*. Instead of going through all the interpretative nuances and disagreements which that position has elicited, I will outline its basic features.

In the original position, parties do not know anything about their conception of the good, their talent, their gender, race, health, etc. By the same token, Rawls notes, they ought not to know which generation they belong to. The question, then, is what they are going to decide when it comes to transfers of wealth from one generation to the next, given that they do not know where they are located in time.

The immediate problem, of course, is that Rawls postulates the parties to be self-interested, and it is unclear, then, why they should care about what happens to their successors. Fortunately, Rawls notes, the parties are heads of families and are therefore concerned with the fate of their children and grandchildren. In particular, they are concerned that the latter should be able to live in a just society. According to Rawls, then, the parties will choose a principle of just savings, the point of which is to preserve just institutions *over time*. As he puts it, the just savings principle is the result of 'an understanding between generations to carry their fair share of the burden of realizing and preserving a just society' (Rawls, 1999a, p. 289). Thus, the principle of just savings is just because it aims at realizing a just society and because each generation must be able to contribute to that project with a fair share of resources.

More precisely, the principle works in two stages. In the first, *accumulation*, stage, a given generation must save and pass on more to its successors than it has received. For if, right from prehistoric times, we held that generations are allowed *not* to save, we would end up in a situation where no accumulation of wealth would occur, and not enough wealth would be created over time to sustain just institutions. However, once just institutions are in place and secure, we reach a *steady-state* stage, where a given generation is not under a duty to save for the sake of its successors. In the accumulation stage, then, savings are mandatory and dis-savings prohibited; in the steady-state stage, savings are no longer mandatory but merely permissible, and dis-savings are still prohibited.

One implication of this view is that, at the accumulation stage, the worst-off members of society, at time t, will be worse off than they would be if their generation did not save for the sake of its successors but instead spent those resources to improve the situation of the worst off. Rawls would argue that this is defensible, if one keeps in mind the necessity of sustaining just institutions in the long run. This in turn presupposes that a minimal amount of wealth is necessary to do just that: empirically, this seems plausible as there appears to be a connection between levels of wealth and the presence, or lack thereof, of strong democratic institutions. It remains to be seen, however, whether a correct understanding of egalitarian justice – and this is what Rawls aims to offer – delivers the conclusion that the current generation must not dis-save, but does not have to save.

We will address this question in section 2.2. For now, note that it brings out the following two aspects of Rawls's account of justice towards future generations. For a start, in so far as the parties are motivated by a concern for the next two generations, the principles which they choose do not address cases where dis-savings will hit their distant successors without hitting their immediate successors. Moreover, Rawls does not regard environmental goods as falling within the remit of justice. From his discussion of public goods in sections 42–3 of *A Theory*, one can infer that environmental goods are public goods, the provision of which cannot be left to the market but must be undertaken by the state. However, they are not primary goods, and their distribution and provision is not a matter for the principles of justice – most notably the difference principle – to decide; it is, rather, a matter for democratic decision-making. As we saw in section 1, however, it is not far-fetched to regard environmental goods as primary goods. For, as we noted there, they can be regarded both as preconditions for enjoying other primary goods (which for Rawls do fall within the scope of justice) and as goods which individuals can and do enjoy in and of themselves. Whether one can construe a Rawlsian theory of environmental justice on that basis remains an interesting question which I will not pursue here.

Before moving on to luck egalitarian accounts of justice towards future generations, it is worth examining the connection between Rawlsian justice and population control, in so far as it highlights a difficulty with Rawls's methodology. Rawls's account of the accumulation and steady-state stages concerns policies such as preserving the environment and saving (or, as the case may be, dis-saving) national wealth. Clearly, though, whether or not future generations will be subject to dis-savings will depend on their size. The question, then, is whether the current generation is under a duty to control the rate of its population growth should it fail not to dis-save wealth, so as to ensure that, at the steady-state stage, future generations are not subject to dis-savings.

Rawls's methodology fails to deliver an answer to that question. As we saw, the parties in the original position do not know which generation they belong to. And it is in ignorance of this fact that they have to decide which policy to adopt towards their successors. In addition, whatever principle they choose will apply to *all* generations. And this is where Rawls's theory seems to encounter an intractable problem. For in so far as whatever principle they decide applies to *all* generations, it applies to the parties' *predecessors* in time. Accordingly, the parties will end up choosing a principle which may result in their own non-existence. Suppose they decide that, as a matter of justice, all generations ought to adopt a one-child only policy. However, to hold the parties' predecessors up to that policy will result in a number of the parties themselves not existing. And that would be conceptually incoherent, since if there is one thing of which the parties can be sure in the original position, it is the fact that they themselves exist.

Let us assume that the foregoing is wrong – that parties in the original position can settle on a principle for population control. Which one would they choose? They would say that individuals are not under an obligation not to reproduce. For, according to Rawls, one cannot sacrifice fundamental rights and liberties for the sake of greater material advantage. In so far as the right to reproduce is a fundamental right, it follows that it cannot be curtailed for the sake of bringing about greater material advantages for our successors. I should say here that luck egalitarians, such as Dworkin, as well as sufficientists (with the notable exception of Brian Barry (Barry, 1999)) would also oppose infringements on the right to reproduce as one wishes. Such infringements, they would claim, constitute an unacceptable violation of bodily and personal integrity. However, Rawlsians, luck egalitarians, and sufficientists can endorse giving individuals incentives to control how many children they have (for example, by publicly funding contraceptive measures and lowering subsidies for childcare, and so on). Their point, then, is that whatever obligations of justice individuals have towards their successors pertain to the environment and wealth, and not to population control.

As we saw in chapter 1, however, some egalitarian liberals argue that a just society is not merely one in which individuals' moral rights against one another are enforced by the law: it is one whose ethos is such that individuals act, in their daily lives, in accordance with the principles of justice, even if their failure so to act would not be sanctioned by the law. On that view, even if it is true that holding individuals under an enforceable obligation not to reproduce as they wish would constitute an unacceptable violation of their autonomy, it might be that they nevertheless are under such a moral obligation. More strongly, they would act unjustly if they failed to fulfil it, even though the law would allow them to do so. In what follows, however, and in so far as egalitarians, liberals (and sufficientists) do not believe that failure to control the rate of population growth is a breach of justice, I will focus on the issues of the environment and economic policies. But it is worth bearing in mind that whether or not we are under an obligation to save material resources (be they natural or man-made), and if so to what extent, will depend on the reproductive decisions we make, within our rights, regarding the size of our successors' generations.

2.2 Luck egalitarianism

As I noted above, Rawls argues that, once the steady-state stage is reached, dis-savings are disallowed, and savings are allowed. It is not clear, however, that other luck egalitarians would agree with him on that score. As we saw in chapter 1, they argue that individuals should not be disadvantaged for reasons which are beyond their control. Accordingly, not only should they not be disadvantaged by their community membership; they should not be disadvantaged by their location in time either.

Now, it seems clear that, on this view, the first generation – G_1 – should not leave less to its successors – G_2 – than it had itself. For were G_1 to dis-save, the members of G_2 would be disadvantaged in virtue of belonging to a generation which comes later in time than a generation – in that instance, G_1 – which chose to dis-save. The question, then, is whether G_1 can, indeed ought to, save, for the sake of G_2. Whichever stand one takes on this will depend on the degree to which one wants principles of justice to be individualistic. If one takes the view that no one should be disadvantaged by factors over which he or she has no control, then it seems that each generation owes at least a fair share to *each individual member* of future generations. This, in turn, suggests that each generation is under an obligation to pass on to its successors the wealth it has itself received, but no more: dis-savings are prohibited but savings are not compulsory. In fact, they are even disallowed, unless every single member of each generation agrees that they should be made. For suppose that G_1 produces a surplus; and suppose that a majority of the members of G_1 decide not to consume it, but instead to pass it on to G_2. G_2 will thus have a greater share than those members of G_1 who would have benefited from the surplus had G_1 decided to keep it for itself. If those members of G_1 did not agree to save this surplus for the sake of G_2, they could complain that they are made worse off than G_2 through no fault of their own (that is, solely in virtue of belonging to a generation, G_1, which has decided to save).

But we might instead think that each generation owes its successors a fair share of economic opportunities, and that it is the responsibility of each generation to ensure that justice obtains between its members. To anticipate somewhat, we will encounter a similar view when discussing global justice in chapter 5. There we will see that national self-determination matters, and that giving it its due is incompatible with the requirement that *no* individual be made worse off for reasons which are beyond his control. Here, we are dealing with the view that *generational* self-determination matters too. On that view, each generation must only ensure that it does not pass on less to its successors than it has itself inherited: savings are allowed, and not mandatory.

The foregoing interpretations of luck egalitarianism are in need of qualification. For a start, those interpretations assume that future generations will not need more resources, to begin with, than we ourselves did. Suppose, however, that we have very strong reasons to believe that a destructive earthquake will occur in about a hundred years from now. Our successors will need far more resources than we started with to deal with the aftermath of the earthquake: they will need to provide health care to the wounded, to rebuild housing, etc. In that case, in so far as, *ex hypothesi*, our successors will not be responsible for their predicament, they have a claim against us that we compensate them, which in turn requires that we set aside at least some of our surplus wealth.

In addition, those interpretations do not take on board the fact that the size of the population is likely to increase over time. Once one takes that fact on board, it is hard to see how we could know what a fair share is, since we simply do not know how many people, in the future, there will be. Simply put, if we do not know how many will want or need to eat the cake, we simply cannot know how to divide the cake. More strongly put, on the plausible assumption that, until our planet ceases to support human life, the total number of individuals among which to divide finite resources will approach infinity, the shares to which they will *all* have a claim will amount to, strictly speaking, nothing.

To conclude, luck egalitarians are not all committed to condoning savings. On an individualistic view of our obligations to future generations, they are more likely to reject savings or, at least, to make savings conditional on the consent of all the members of the generation whose savings it is. On a more collective view of our obligations, savings are allowed but not mandatory, unless we know that our successors will need that extra surplus through no fault of their own.

2.3 Sufficiency

The difficulty which population size poses for luck egalitarians is one reason why some people of a strongly egalitarian bent are tempted to adopt a sufficientist view of our obligations to our successors. According to sufficiency theorists, you recall, what matters is not that individuals should not be worse off than others through no fault of their own; what matters is that they have enough resources. If having enough means ensuring that one's basic needs are met, then all we must do is ensure that our successors have enough resources not to be utterly destitute. Deciding how much to save for that purpose is much easier than working out how much to save to ensure that our successors each have an equal share. Put differently, the difficulties raised by extending the scope of justice to future generations have led some to revise their understanding of the content of justice.

This, of course, does not provide a sufficientist *justification* for these particular obligations. On what grounds, then, would sufficiency theorists defend obligations to future generations? They believe that individuals should not be left below the sufficiency threshold for reasons which are outside their control – such as race, gender, disability. They also believe, more simply, that acting in such a way as to seriously harm others is morally wrong. As a result, they are committed to the view that individuals should not be left below the threshold simply in virtue of the fact that they are born at a particular time, and that the current generation simply ought not to act in such a way as to seriously harm its successors. From a sufficientist viewpoint, then, economic and social policy should be such as to ensure that future generations have enough. Ideas such as sustainable development are very much in line with a sufficientist view of distributive justice (Dobson, 1998).

On closer inspection, however, and with one qualification to be made below, the position is not that radical. As we noted in chapter 1, defining the meaning of 'having enough' is one of sufficientists' toughest challenges. Frankfurt claims that to have enough means having enough to implement one's basic, reasonable, aims. As to Anderson, she argues that having enough means having the resources necessary to function as a full citizen in a social democracy. But above and beyond basic needs, it is quite hard to see what is required for people to fulfil their basic ends, or to function as full citizens. And it is even harder to make that judgement, of course, where future generations are concerned, for we simply do not know what will be required, in a hundred years from now, to be a full citizen in a social democracy or, indeed, to implement one's basic and reasonable aims. We do not know that, because what will be required will depend in large part on the kind of society in which our successors will live, and we have no means of knowing what *that* will be like. Accordingly, sufficientists have to fall back on the view that each generation must ensure that its successors can meet their basic needs for food, water, minimum health, etc. Sufficiency, in this context, simply does mean meeting basic needs (Barry, 1999).

As indicated above, however, the foregoing point is subject to the following qualification, which stems from the capabilities approach we outlined in chapter 1. When used in a sufficientist theory of justice, the capabilities approach, you recall, lists a number of human capabilities, and argues that individuals owe it to one another, as a matter of justice, to ensure that they all possess the freedoms and resources required for the enjoyment of a basic threshold of those capabilities. If, as some proponents of the approach have suggested, it is plausible to assert that among all human capabilities is the capacity to have a rich and fulfilling relationship to the environment, then justice requires that we not deprive our successors of environmental goods so understood – that we do not, for example, spoil areas of great natural beauty (Nussbaum, 2000).

Setting aside those difficulties, sufficientists can quite easily endorse the following views: (1) G_1 is not *required* to save for the sake of its successors, if whatever it leaves them suffices to meet their basic needs. (2) More controversially, G_1 is allowed to pass on to its successors less than what it inherited (thus, to dis-save), provided that future generations would still have their basic needs met (Barry, 1999).

Whether G_1 has the right to save for the sake of its successors is a trickier issue, particularly when its successors do not exist yet (G_3). According to sufficientists, one should give priority to those who are the closest to reaching the sufficiency threshold. In so far as individuals who currently exist are closer to reaching the threshold than individuals who do not as yet exist, it seems that G_1's poor members have priority over G_3. However, this argument is too quick. Take the case of a member of G_1 who suffers from a long-term, degenerative, and severe disease for which there is no cure. Contrast his plight with the plight of a member of G_3, who will suffer from hunger unless she gets extra resources. It is not clear that the member of G_1 is closer to reaching the sufficiency threshold than the member of G_3, and it is not clear, therefore, that he should get extra resources to the detriment of the latter. In fact, it seems that, at the bar of sufficiency, the destitute member of G_3 has a much stronger claim. If sufficientists wish to maintain that priority should be given to those who have the greatest chance of having their needs met, then it seems that, in some cases, they will have to commit themselves to the view not merely that G_1 has the right to save for the sake of its successors, but also that it is under an obligation to do so, and this to the detriment of some of its members.

3 The transgenerational community: a source of obligations to our successors

In section 2, I outlined the bare bones of luck egalitarian and suffic-ientist theories of justice towards future generations. In this section, I describe a communitarian account of it. If anything, the task at hand is harder than it was then, as avowedly communitarian philosophers have not taken an explicit stand on this difficult issue. In fact, on some communitarian meta-ethical views of how to derive principles of justice, it does seem as if we cannot, in fact, construct a theory of our obligations to our successors. Remember Sandel's claim, for example, to the effect that it does not make sense to derive conclusions about what justice requires of us by appealing to the choices which individ-uals would make, behind a veil of ignorance of their specific charac-teristics and in abstraction from the social environment in which they live. Remember, too, Walzer's particularistic understanding of justice, whereby justice is rooted in the distinct understandings of places, honours, jobs, and all those things which constitute a shared way of life. Those of our successors who do not as yet exist do not fit easily in either account. For if principles of justice are shaped in, and by, the social, political, economic, and cultural environment in which the individuals to which they apply live, then we – here and now – who do not know what our successors' environment will look like two hundred years from now simply cannot know how we should behave towards them.

As we noted in chapter 1, however, this particular, meta-theoretical understanding of justice is not all that there is to communitarianism. According to Sandel, McIntyre, and Taylor, Rawlsian liberalism is to be charged for arguing, unwarrantedly, that individuals are not under obligations which they do not voluntarily endorse. In fact, they argue, we do have obligations which we have not chosen, and we have them in virtue of shared membership in a particular institution, such as the family or the community. While none of those three thinkers has offered a full account of justice towards our successors, an interesting defence of obligations to future generations which appeals to com-munal obligations of that kind has been deployed by Avner de-Shalit (de-Shalit, 1995). Human beings, he argues, belong to a community of moral values, language, culture, history, traditions, etc., and this even though they do not interact with one another on a daily basis. By the same token, then, we should see that it is not necessary for indi-viduals to belong to the same community, that they should coexist in time. Moreover, just as a community extends to the past, it also extends to the future: the English know, for example, that there will still be a recognizably English community a hundred years from now. In that sense, individuals belong to local and national, but also *transgenerational*, communities. And if they ought to ensure that fellow community members, say, their fellow English contemporaries, are not harmed by their policies, and receive help (as the communitarian argument under study assumes), then they also ought to ensure that future English people are not harmed by them. As de-Shalit notes, his conclusion receives support from the fact that individuals do care about what happens to their successors.

The notion of a transgenerational community and of the obligations it generates does not tell us what those obligations are. It does not tell us, for example, whether G_1 should control the rate of its population growth; nor does it tell us whether we should look to the idea of sustainable development when delineating what G_1 owes to its successors. Put differently, it tells us about the scope of justice, but not about its content. What it seeks to provide, instead, is a basis for the general claim that G_1 has communal obligations to its successors. Moreover, as a communitarian theory of justice, it goes against recent trends, both within and without academia, to couch obligations to others in the language of rights. Thus, according to communitarians (or so I surmise), one cannot counter a putative charge that G_1 ought to control the rate of its population growth by invoking the view that its members have the right to reproduce as they wish (as libertarians and most liberals would do). For rights, McIntyre would reiterate, are nothing but chimera for which no rational argument can be found; and were such an argument to be found, Sandel might press, it is unclear that rights always trump community values such as attachment to the welfare of one's successors.

As a justification for our obligations to future generations, the notion of a transgenerational community works better in the case of overlapping generations than it does in the case of more distant generations. For, obviously, the further forward one goes in time, the more a given community changes. England is very different in 2007 from what it was in 1907. Its ethnic composition has changed radically in the last hundred years, and its infinitely more diverse population holds values and principles (on the role of women, the acceptance of homosexuals, etc.) which were anathema at the turn of the twentieth century. It is unclear, then, how the notion of transgenerational community can justify the claim that the generation of English people who lived a century ago might have had an obligation to the current generation of English people. Likewise, it is likely that the community which will live on this territory a hundred years from now will be very different, culturally and socially, from the current English community. Accordingly, it is unclear why the latter has obligations to its distant successors.

A natural response to this worry is to say, not implausibly, that our obligations to future generations simply fade over time. The problem, though, is that many of the effects of our policies will be felt, precisely, by distant generations, particularly with respect to the environment. To give but two examples, the nuclear waste which we are currently dumping may not start leaking radioactive elements for another two or three hundred years. Likewise, climatic changes triggered by rapid industrialization may have the most impact three or four generations down the line.

In addition, many of those effects will be felt by members of communities which are different from ours not merely because they are remote in time, but also because they are located on a different territory. The case of Chernobyl is paradigmatic of the problem: the effect of the explosion that took place in this Ukrainian nuclear plant in 1985 was felt hundreds of miles away. Consider, too, the case of the deforestation of the Amazon area, which is widely thought to contribute to the thinning of the ozone layer. Accept, further, with a number of scientists, that the thinning of the ozone layer contributes to the progressive melting of the ice caps, rising tides, the gradual erosion of coastlines in Northern Europe, and so on. Under such conditions, the notion of a transgenerational community alone does not seem to be able to support the view that the current generations which live in communities around the Amazon are under an obligation to distant generations of, say, England and the Netherlands. It seems, in other words, that one cannot address the question of our obligations to future generations without, also, addressing the question of our obligations to foreigners (Beckerman and Pasek, 2001).

4 Libertarianism and future generations

Let us turn, finally, to libertarianism, starting with population control. As we saw in chapter 1, libertarians believe that we have unrestricted rights of ownership over our own body. This, in turn, implies that we, and only we, decide whether, and how, to use our body's reproductive capacities: we can reproduce as we wish, and have however many children we wish. Quite straightforwardly, then, libertarians deny that we are under an obligation of justice to control the rate of population growth. To put the point differently, our successors do not have the right that we desist from reproducing as we wish.

Matters are not so straightforward, however, when it comes to whatever obligations G_1 has, if any, to its successors with respect to the wealth it creates and the natural environment in which it lives. In fact, the conclusions to which libertarians arrive on these two issues in part depend on the theory of rights which they endorse. Before I make my case to that effect, a point of terminology is in order. Libertarians, you recall, argue that *individuals* have unrestricted ownership rights over themselves and over legitimately acquired property. They reject the view that groups have rights. Accordingly, in what follows, when I talk of the current generation, or when I say 'G_1', I will mean 'individual members of G_1'. This is not to say that there is no sense in which we can talk of a generation as a group, within a libertarian framework. It is to say, rather, that, on the libertarian view, whatever collective decisions are made by those individuals must receive the consent of all, on pain of breaching the self-ownership rights of the dissenters.

Now, of all the competing theories of rights, two stand out for their sophistication and popularity. According to the so-called choice-based theory of rights, famously articulated by H. L. A. Hart, to say that an agent, A, has a right that another agent, B, do or do not P, means that A is able to demand, or waive, B's performance of her duty (Hart, 1955). For example, to say that A has a right to freedom of speech against B is to say that A can demand that B let him speak, or can allow B to censor him. According to the so-called interest-based theory of rights, famously articulated, among others, by Joseph Raz, for A to have a right that B do or do not P, means that an interest of A's is strong enough to warrant holding B under a duty to do, or not do, P (Raz, 1986). On that view, to say that A has a right to freedom of speech against B is to say that A's interest in freedom of speech is important enough to impose on B a duty to let A speak.

Although there is nothing in libertarianism which commits its proponents to endorsing either one or the other of those two theories of rights, historically, they have adopted the choice-based theory of rights, which has the following implications for their understanding of our obligations to future generations. For a start, in so far as to have a right, on this view, means that one is able to waive or demand the performance of the correlative duties, distant generations simply cannot, and do not, have any rights at all against the latter. Whatever obligations of justice G_1 has are owed to generations which already exist – extending, thus, to its great-grandchildren at the most.

With that important qualification in hand, let us now assess which obligations any given generation – G – has to its successors thus defined. As I noted in section 1, we need to distinguish between saving, or dis-saving, the wealth we create, and preserving, or spoiling, the natural resources which we use in order to create wealth. And it is this last point which somewhat complicates the Lockean-inspired libertarian picture, as drawn by Nozick. For Nozick, you recall (and indeed most libertarians), does not subscribe to the view that working on natural resources is enough to justify unlimited property rights in them: it is enough *provided* that one does not worsen other people's situation by doing so. As Nozick points out, the proviso takes a weak as well as a strong form. On the strong version, appropriation is legitimate only if it does not worsen other people's opportunities to appropriate things. On the weak form, appropriation is legitimate only if it does not worsen other people's opportunities to use things.

As applied to contemporaries, the proviso seems simple enough. As applied to successive generations, it is more problematic. It stipulates, in that case, that any given generation has the right to appropriate land and natural resources, provided it does not worsen its successors' opportunities to appropriate, or to use, those resources. On the strong form of the proviso, this suggests that, when G_1 appropriates natural resources, it must leave as much for its successors to appropriate as it itself had. On the weak form, G must ensure that its successors have equal opportunities to use natural resources, or to use the equivalent of such resources. This, in turn, implies that G_1 is not allowed to waste or consume non-renewable natural resources unless it ensures that they are replaced with resources of a similar kind, or which bring similar benefits. Consider the case of oil, as an example. On the libertarian view, if we use up current reserves of oil, we must ensure that we develop alternative sources of energy for our successors. Waste without proper compensation, then, is prohibited.

So much, then, for natural resources. But what about the wealth which a generation creates with them? In so far as individuals enjoy full ownership rights over their labour, they can decide to spend the product of their labour as they wish, and thus are not under any obligation to their successors to pass it on to them. In fact, and more strongly (or so a libertarian wedded to the choice-based theory of rights would argue), G lacks the right to pass on its surplus wealth to its successors. For consider: on this view of rights, for A to have a right to bequeath his property to B means that A can choose to demand that third parties let B become the owner of his property, or to allow them not to do so. Now, third parties are under that duty to the testator only once he is dead; for it is only then that the transfer of rights to the heir designated by the will can take place, and that the issue of whether one should let it go ahead can arise. In so far as dead people cannot, logically, demand or waive the fulfilment of duties, then they do not have a right to bequeath their property. In the present context, those libertarians would maintain, G does not have the right to hand over its wealth to its successors: savings – understood, here, as transferring one's ownership rights over the wealth one has created to one's successors – are disallowed (Steiner, 1994).

The foregoing, note, implies that G_1 is allowed to consume the whole of the wealth it has created. But it does not imply that it *must* do so. Indeed, the claim that G_1 cannot bequeath its savings to its successors simply means that it cannot transfer ownership rights over its savings and is fully compatible with the view that G_1 is permitted to leave surplus wealth behind. On the libertarian view described here, the surplus wealth created and left by G_1 should be regarded as having the same status as natural resources before they are appropriated – that is to say, unowned, and there for G_1's successors to appropriate as a matter of (equal) right.

To recapitulate, then, libertarians who endorse the choice-based theory of rights hold that dis-savings are allowed, that G_1 lacks the right to pass on its wealth to its successors, and that it is under an obligation to generations which overlap with it, but not to distant generations, not to waste natural resources without due compensation.

As I noted above, however, libertarians are not committed, by virtue of their libertarianism, to the choice-based theory of rights. Should they endorse the interest-based theory instead, they would not rule out from the outset the possibility that distant generations can have rights against current generations. For, after all, future people, even if they do not exist, might be supposed to have interests that warrant protection. Suppose, then, that those libertarians are correct in holding (a) that individuals own themselves as well as the product of their labour, (b) that appropriation is legitimate subject to the Lockean proviso, and (c) that non-existing people can have rights. On that view, the precise location in time of future generations in relation to G_1 is irrelevant to determining the latter's obligations, should it have any. Thus, in so far as those libertarians hold (b) and (c), they are committed to the view that future generations, whether or not they overlap with G_1, have a right against the latter that it not waste natural resources without proper compensation. They are also committed to the view that G_1 is under an obligation to ensure, upon appropriating land and natural resources, that it does not worsen its distant successors' opportunities to appropriate or to use resources (on the strong or weak interpretations of the proviso respectively). In addition, in so far as they hold (a), they are committed to the view that G_1 has the right *not* to pass on the wealth it has created to its successors, since rights over one's labour include a right to consume the product of one's labour in its entirety.

Before concluding, there is a further issue to consider. G_1, the current generation, which exists here and now, has predecessors, G_0, who are now dead, and whose surplus wealth G_1 has inherited. The question, then, is whether G_1 has the right not to pass on G_0's wealth to its own successors (G_2, G_3, etc.). This in fact depends on G_0's declared intentions. Suppose that G_0 has made no explicit decision as to how its surplus wealth should be allocated once it has ceased to exist. It seems that, in that case, libertarians who endorse the interest-based theory of rights would argue that the wealth should be regarded as unowned by anyone, and that members of G_1 can appropriate it if, and only if, they do not thereby worsen their successors' opportunities to appropriate or use resources in general, whether their successors already exist or not. Suppose, by contrast, that G_0 did make a decision as to how the wealth it had created should be distributed once it had ceased to exist: for example, it decided that G_1 should benefit from it. In that case, all G_1 needs to do, vis-à-vis its successors, is to ensure that it does not appropriate as yet unowned natural resources if it would thereby worsen their opportunities. In so far as it has rightfully inherited the wealth created by G_0, it enjoys full rights of ownership over it, and is not, therefore, under any obligation to pass it on to G_{2-n}.

To recapitulate, on the interest-based theory of rights, libertarianism holds that any generation is under an obligation of justice not to waste natural resources without compensation, irrespective of the location in time of its successors. It also holds that any given generation has the right both to save and to dis-save the wealth it has created and/or inherited from its predecessors.

5 Future generations and the non-identity objection

We have reviewed a number of positions on justice towards future generations. All of them argue that any given generation is under some obligations to its successors – ranging from obligations not to waste natural resources without proper compensation to obligations to pass on surplus wealth in some cases, and so on. In some – but not all – cases, the views on offer either explicitly claim, or imply, that future generations have rights against the current generation. Whether or not non-existing people can have rights is a hotly debated issue which I will not address here (Buchanan et al., 2000; Dobson, 1998; Vanderheiden, 2006). Instead, I look at an important objection to the view that we have obligations to our successors, namely the so-called non-identity objection, famously articulated and explored by Derek Parfit (Parfit, 1984, chs. 16–17). The objection goes like this. The view at issue says the following:

> G_1 has to choose between, say, depleting natural resources and pre-serving them. If it does the latter, it will leave its successors, individual members of a future generation, say G_3, worse off than they would be if it chose the latter policy. Or, on a sufficientist interpretation, it would make it much more difficult for them to meet their basic needs than would be the case if it preserved those resources. Thus, G_1 will harm G_3 by choosing to deplete, rather than preserve, natural resources; it is therefore under an obligation to G_3 to choose the latter course of action.

As the non-identity objection notes, this view compares the fate of individual members of G_3 under a depletion policy with their fate under a preservation policy. However, the objection continues, this comparison is not possible, in so far as the genetic identity of individual members of G_3 will change depending on which policy G_1 adopts. For consider: our genetic identity – whether we are the individual known as Peter or the individual known as Mary – depends on our parents' genetic identity as well as on when they have sexual intercourse. Of every one of us, it is true that, if the sexual intercourse between our parents which resulted in our conception had not taken place pretty much exactly when it took place, we would not have been conceived: in other words, we simply would not exist. This is because a woman's individual egg can only be fertilized within a two- to three-day window once it has descended into her fallopian tubes; and a man's spermatozoa remain alive, once in a woman's body, for about twenty-four hours only. In fact, even if our parents had had intercourse, not when we were in fact conceived, but, say, twenty hours later, it is very unlikely that the *same* spermatozoon would have fertilized that egg, and it is very unlikely, therefore, that we would exist.

At this point, what, one may ask, does that have to do with justice to future generations? Quite simply this: foreign, economic and social policies shape our opportunities for work and for moving around. They in turn affect where we live and whom we meet. As a result, they affect when, and with whom, we have sexual intercourse, and thereby the very identity of our children, which has an impact on the identity of our grandchildren, great-grandchildren, and so on.

How does this bear on the question of justice towards future generations? I have outlined above a set of obligations to future generations to which egalitarian liberals, indeed some communitarians and libertarians, are committed. On their views, G_1 would harm, and in fact *wrong*, future generations if it did not conduct the required policies. However, the non-identity objection suggests that, *if* it fails to conduct those policies, it will cause individual members of those future generations to exist who would not have existed had it conducted such policies. Consider the following example. Suppose that G_1 conducts a policy of heavy industrialization which causes very severe pollution, but which also creates jobs and contributes to expanding town suburbs in a given area. Had it opted for an environment-friendly policy instead, individuals who met as a result of the creation of those jobs would not have produced the children that they in fact conceived; and those children, in turn, would not have produced the descendants who are now adversely affected by the pollution. Different – that is, genetically different – individuals would have been created instead. According to the non-identity objection, in so far as individual members of future generations would not have existed otherwise, they have not been harmed by G_1's failure not to pollute. And if that is true, then they have not been wronged by G_1, which implies that G_1 was not under an obligation to them, in the first instance, not to pollute.

What are we to make of this? There are two ways – one interesting, the other not – in which that objection is construed. Let me first dispose of the uninteresting construal. For some people, giving life to someone cannot be wrongful to that person, because life is better than non-existence. This construal of the objection is uninteresting, in so far as it rests on the wildly implausible view that life *no matter its quality* is worth having. Yet it seems uncontroversial to say that non-existence is better than some kinds of life. Thus, policies which cause individual members of future generations to lead their whole life on the verge of starvation or to die of pollution-induced diarrhoea at the age of five do harm them, even though they cause them to exist. In fact, one might plausibly argue that those policies harm those individuals to such an extent that G_1 is under an obligation to them to choose a different course of action, at the cost, as it were, of those individuals' existence.

The objection is more interesting in those cases where G_1's failure to conduct, say, environment-friendly policies results in members of future generations leading a life of poverty, but nevertheless one worth living. For, in those cases, we can say that life under those circumstances is better than non-existence or, at any rate, that it is not worse than non-existence. And if life is not worse than non-existence, then it seems – if the objection is correct – that individual members of future generations who owe their life to environmentally unfriendly policies cannot complain that they have been made worse off. As a result, it is not true that they have been harmed; and it is not true, therefore, that they have been wronged. They certainly cannot complain that their rights have been violated.

The non-identity objection has generated a voluminous body of literature, which it is beyond the scope of this chapter to explore. Let me simply make a few comments. For a start, I am assuming here (and will continue to assume) that, even though the policies which G_1 conducts affect the identities of G_1's successors, they do not at the same time affect the size of these generations. As we saw earlier, none of the various theories of justice we examined here accept that we are under an obligation of justice to reduce the size of future generations by controlling the rate of our own population growth. I will not, therefore, deal with the non-identity objection as raised against the view that we ought to act in such a way.

Moreover, the non-identity objection applies only to policies which affect the identity of our successors. It does not affect policies which 'merely' harm them. Suppose that G_1 decides to encase nuclear waste in concrete and to bury it, several hundred feet deep, in a remote, desert area, with no maintenance (and thus no human activity) required. Three hundred years down the line, the area is hit by an earthquake, as a result of which the concrete fractures and the nuclear waste starts leaking into the phreatic table, thereby contaminating water supplies in densely populated areas 300 miles away. In so acting, G_1 did not cause human beings to exist which would otherwise not have existed, and a claim to the effect that it was under an obligation not to dump the waste is not vulnerable in any way to the non-identity objection.

Having said that, most of the policies conducted by any given generation do affect the identities of its successors. Is this to say, then, that G_1 simply cannot be held under any obligation to its successors, provided that it does not act in such a way as to make their life less than worth living? Not necessarily. In fact, there are at least two problems which proponents of the non-identity objection would have to deal with. First, they may well err in thinking that, when assessing our obligations to others, the latter's genetic identity matters. It could very well be that we owe certain things to future people, *whoever they are*. On that view, whoever they are, we have an obligation to ensure that they have clean water, adequate nutrition, etc.

Let me put the point differently. The non-identity objection assumes that, when we delineate our obligations to others, we should adopt the so-called person-affecting principle, whereby P harms Q by doing A if A makes Q worse off than he would have been had P not done A. The principle is person-affecting in that it supposes that the genetic identity of the persons to which it applies remains the same. The non-identity objection claims that the principle cannot apply to *non-identity* cases, where Q would not exist but for the fact that P did A, since Q is not worse off for existing. However, if we drop the requirement that our obligations to others take a person-affecting form, if, instead, we accept that we have impersonal obligations, then we are in a position to say that we have an obligation to ensure that future generations are not made worse off, or needy, whoever they are.

Second, assume that identity does matter. Still, this would not rescue the objection. For the objection rests on a concealed and questionable premise, namely that, in judging whether the current generation's policy vis-à-vis future generations is morally wrong, one must assess whether the policy negatively or positively affects the quality of future generations' life *overall*. And yet, even if one does not make future generations worse off overall, one can still harm a *particular* interest of theirs. Suppose that an airline refuses to sell a ticket to Smith on a given flight, on the grounds that Smith is black. Smith cannot board that flight, which, as it happens, crashes, killing all on board. Clearly, the airline did not make Smith worse off by refusing to sell him that ticket. However, they did harm one of his fundamental interests, that is, his interest in not being discriminated against on grounds of race. In so acting, the airline failed to regard him as having equal worth and thereby infringed his right to be treated with equal respect (Woodward, 1986). One can deploy a similar argument in the present context: perhaps our current policies cause certain future individuals to exist and live a life worth living, albeit one characterized by poverty. But even if they are better off overall (or at least not worse off) for living such a life, it may still be that we harm some interests of theirs in not ensuring that they have a minimally decent standard of living. And so it may still be that we wrong them by failing so to act.

6 Conclusion

In this chapter, we have reviewed communitarian, libertarian, Rawlsian, egalitarian, and sufficientist positions on the very difficult issue of justice towards future generations. In each case, we have seen that it was necessary to distinguish between various ways in which we – the current generation – are in a position to harm our successors: environmental policies, policies relating to the accumulation or waste of national wealth, and population policies. Whether or not we do have obligations to our distant successors depends, in part, on the size of the population, the extent to which needs or equality are met within our own generation, and the strength of the non-identity objection.

3 Multiculturalism

1 Introduction

In chapter 2, we relaxed the assumption that principles of justice delineate what *contemporaries* owe to one another. In this chapter, we will examine accounts of justice which take seriously the fact of cultural, ethnic, and religious diversity. Indeed, most of us live in societies made up of individuals from different countries, different religions, and different ethnic groups, and with different sexual orientations – individuals, in short, from different *groups*. Many of those groups constitute minorities and stand in conflict with the majority of the population. For example, Catholics, Muslims, and Jews are each a minority in the United Kingdom; so are Christians in Saudi Arabia, Russians in the Ukraine, and homosexuals in all countries. The question, then, is that of the social arrangements which a polity ought to adopt in the face of its diversity.

As a matter of fact, minorities often complain that they are being treated unfairly by the majority. There are at least five kinds of claim which those groups make:

1　a claim to the effect that their individual members should have the same rights as the individual members of the majority. For example, in some countries such as Britain and the USA, homosexuals have asked to be given the right to marry. In nineteenth-century Europe, Jews demanded to have the same rights of citizenship as Gentiles.
2　a claim to be exempt, on religious or cultural grounds, from obligations which members of the majority, or indeed from other groups, have to fulfil. In the UK, for example, Sikhs have asked to be exempt from having to wear a helmet while riding a motorcycle or working on building sites.

3 a claim for extra resources to subsidize those goods which are culturally important to them. For example, in some countries, linguistic minorities are asking their government for extra subsidies towards the teaching of their (minority) languages. Thus, in the 1960s and 1970s, Welsh activists campaigned, in the end successfully, for the provision of Welsh teaching in primary and secondary schools.

4 a claim for special representation rights in political institutions. Thus, it is sometimes argued that a legislative assembly ought to reserve a number of its seats for underprivileged and minority groups, on the grounds that the latter's interests are not served well enough under a culture-neutral system of representation. For example, in Pakistan, Iran, and Bangladesh, non-Muslims have reserved parliamentary seats; so do Maoris in New Zealand.

5 a claim for special rights of national self-government, falling short of secession. Thus, Scotland and Wales in the UK, Catalonia in Spain, and Quebec in Canada have obtained some degree of autonomy from central government, on *national* grounds.

The first claim is a demand for an extension of universal rights; the other four are demands for *special* rights. I will focus on special rights, as they are harder to justify than the claim that one should not be treated unequally for arbitrary reasons such as gender, religion, and sexual orientation. My aim is to review what some liberals, communitarians, and libertarians have to say about demands for special rights, and to address the following questions: Do those claims vary in strength? Does it make sense to understand them as group rights? Are there differences between demands made by national groups (the French in Canada, the Catalonians in Spain, the Russians in the Ukraine even) and demands made by groups of immigrants? Proponents of special rights tend to think that national groups have stronger claims than immigrants. Is that correct?

2 An egalitarian liberal position: Kymlicka's defence of minority rights

No account of minority claims can avoid discussing the groundbreaking works by the Canadian philosopher Will Kymlicka on the issues raised above (Kymlicka, 1989, 1995). Not only was he the first to offer a systematic theory of justice towards cultural and ethnic minorities; he is also one of the few egalitarian liberal advocates of rights for minorities. In this section, we examine his arguments in defence of those rights, as deployed in his *Multicultural Citizenship* (Kymlicka, 1995).

Kymlicka's defence centres around three distinctions and three arguments. First, he distinguishes between rights to special representation in political institutions (as per (4) above), self-government rights (as per (5) above), and polyethnic rights (as per (2) and (3) above). Second, and relatedly, those rights can serve two functions. On the one hand, they give minority groups *external protection* from interference on the part of the larger group; on the other hand, they enable them to impose *internal restrictions* on the freedom of their own individual members (Kymlicka, 1995, p. 7). According to Kymlicka, an egalitarian liberal theory of minority rights is one in which minorities are given external protection if, and only if, they do not use them as a means to oppress their own members. Third, he distinguishes between national minorities, such as French Québécois in Canada, and immigrants, such as Turks in Germany. As we will see, on his view, the former ought to enjoy rights of special representation and self-government, whereas the latter have no such claim.

Kymlicka deploys three arguments in support of minority rights: the equality justification; the justification from historical agreement; and the justification from the value of cultural diversity. Let us begin with the first justification, which is also the most important of all three. Individual autonomy – the capacity to frame, revise, and pursue a conception of the good life – is a fundamentally important value which the state must promote and protect. It does so by conferring on individuals a vast range of rights and freedoms. In particular, the state must ensure that individuals have *equal* opportunities to be autonomous, in the Dworkinian sense that they ought not to be disadvantaged for reasons which are beyond their control. Put differently, unchosen inequalities which result from cultural membership ought to be redressed.

Now, access to what Kymlicka calls a 'societal culture' – encompassing language, a shared history, and cultural goods, as well as a range of political and social institutions – is a necessary precondition for individual autonomy. As Kymlicka argues, one cannot frame, revise, and pursue a conception of the good in isolation from the culture into which one is born. As it happens, some cultures – minority cultures – are in danger of disappearing, through no fault of their members, unless they are given special protection. In so far as the inequalities that arise between members of those minority cultures and members of the majority are beyond the former's control, justice requires that the state protect them, by granting them special rights.

Note that the equality argument seems to support all three kinds of rights. Quite straightforwardly, it seems to support cultural and religious exemptions from the law. In the UK, for example, the law stipulates that one cannot ride a motorcycle without wearing a helmet. According to the equality argument, the law places at an unchosen disadvantage those who, for religious reasons, have to wear a turban and who thus cannot wear a helmet. Moreover, the equality argument also seems to support special representation rights, as well as rights to self-government, in so far as those rights enable minorities 'to protect [their] interests in culture-affecting decisions' (Kymlicka, 1995, p. 113). Interestingly, this particular justification for special representation rights differs from the more traditional argument that individuals ought to be represented by those who share their most fundamental characteristics such as race, gender, etc. As Kymlicka points out, the 'mirror argument', if pushed to its logical conclusion, seems to render any form of representation incoherent, first, because groups overlap along dimensions such as gender and race, and second, because individual members of any group will substantially differ from one another as well (ibid., ch. 7). Far better to conceive of special representation rights as a temporary measure for eradicating oppression, and to be aware of their limits (How many seats ought groups to be guaranteed? Which groups ought to be represented? How are group representatives to be held accountable?, etc.).

The second justification for minority rights invokes the importance of respecting historical agreements. Suppose that a state was formed between two national groups by way of a treaty outlining rights and privileges over land, decision-making powers, etc. If one of those groups becomes a majority in that state, it must not rescind the terms of that treaty, first, because it is on those terms that the state acquired authority over its constituent members, and second, because, in signing that agreement, the majority created in the minority a legitimate expectation that it would abide by its terms. Although historical agreements of that kind are more likely to justify political rights of special representation and self-government, they can also justify polyethnic rights. As Kymlicka notes, the Christian Hutterite sect was granted a number of exemption rights (to do with education and landownership) when they settled in Western Canada. Were the Canadian state to abrogate those rights, the Hutterites would have a legitimate grievance since they would not have settled in that province under different terms.

Kymlicka's third argument for minority rights pertains to the value of cultural diversity. As he puts it, 'cultural diversity is said to be valuable, both in the quasi-aesthetic sense that it creates a more interesting world, and because other cultures contain alternative models of social organization that may be useful in adapting to new circumstances' (1995, p. 121). As he also notes, however, this particular argument is less likely to support rights to special representation and self-government. For the benefits which the majority would derive from living in a state whose diversity is protected by those rights are rather diffuse, and might well be outweighed by their attendant costs. Thus, it is unclear that an Anglophone living in Quebec would accede, on the grounds of the value of diversity, to French Québécois' demand that all provincial government jobs should go to French speakers. By contrast, polyethnic rights protect cultural diversity much more directly, and at a lesser cost to majority members.

In the remainder of this section, I will discuss three aspects of Kymlicka's defence of minority rights: the distinction he draws between national minorities and immigrants; his appeal to the value of equality; and the problem of illiberal minorities.

At various junctures in *Multicultural Citizenship*, Kymlicka makes it clear that immigrants do not have the same range of rights against the majority as national minorities. Remember his understanding of culture. As we saw above, Kymlicka says that we need access to a societal culture in order to be truly autonomous. The question, then, is why we need access to the culture into which we are born rather than to any societal culture. After all, one might argue, people do move between cultures, and it therefore does not seem illegitimate to expect them to integrate into the mainstream culture, even if they have a societal culture of their own.

But the reason why this would be illegitimate, Kymlicka argues, is that such a move is usually very costly. People do not in fact move from one culture to the next easily (contrary to what some liberals, usually academics who are used to moving from one country to the next, like to believe). And we should not *expect* them to do so unless they choose to do so. If he is right, though, he needs to define culture in such a way as to distinguish those cultures which can conceivably be regarded as giving rise to special claims and those cultures which cannot do so. Kymlicka restricts the former to societal cultures, which provide their members with 'meaningful ways of life across the full range of human activities, including social, educational, religious, recreational, and economic life, encompassing both public and private sphere' (1995, p. 76). So, a football fan cannot claim that football is centrally important to his culture, and that he should get subsidies to buy a full season ticket to watch his favourite football club. On the face of it, this sounds plausible enough. However, considerations such as these lead Kymlicka to differentiate between *national communities*, which already have a full societal culture within the larger community, and *immigrants*, which lack such culture. As has often been argued, such differentiation is problematic.

In Kymlicka's view, not only do national communities (such as Québécois in Canada) have some rights to political self-determination within the larger community – something which immigrants lack; they also have stronger claims to special provision and exemption from the law. In particular, they can rightfully demand that the larger community should pay for the provision of public services in their own language, whereas immigrants cannot make that demand. All the latter can claim are some special rights such as exemptions from various laws which regulate when shops must close (usually on Sundays, to the detriment of Muslims and Jews), or what kind of protective headgear cyclists or construction workers must wear (helmets, to the detriment of Sikhs).

Kymlicka's basis for making such a distinction between national communities and immigrants is that the former are the descendants of colonists who aimed at systematically re-creating a society in a new land, whereas immigrants make a decision to join an already existing society. Proponents of special rights for immigrants are not likely to find this line of argument convincing, simply because many immigrants do not really choose to leave their own country. More often than not, their decision is forced on them by their own government's policies, or indeed policies undertaken by international institutions (political persecution, dire poverty, etc.). Kymlicka acknowledges this, and responds that host governments cannot be asked realistically to help all the victims of such unjust policies. Unfortunately, this does not sit very well with his egalitarian liberal views on unchosen disadvantages. After all, we do not say to children whose parents have abused them that, as that injustice was committed by someone else, we, the larger community, are not under an obligation to pick up the tab. Why treat involuntary immigrants differently, then?

The case of immigrant communities whose members did not settle abroad as a result of persecution or dire poverty is also problematic.

Suppose that the Indian community in the UK was territorially concentrated, and that its members demanded rights to self-government short of secession. Why not accede to their request? Because – Kymlicka argues – they came here voluntarily (let us assume) in the knowledge that they would succeed by integrating themselves into mainstream society. But note that, even if the first generation of immigrants did come voluntarily, their children, who were born here, clearly did not. Interestingly, in liberal countries, it is often second and third generations of immigrants who are distancing themselves from the prevailing Western culture, and seeking to 'return' to their parents' roots. And it is not clear why their demand for some political rights of self-determination and representation – should they make such demands – should not be taken seriously.

The second aspect of Kymlicka's argument which warrants further scrutiny is his appeal to equality. In fact, some avowedly liberal commentators dispute that the value of equality can justify special rights, particularly exemptions from the law. Return to the case of the Sikhs. As noted, in the UK, motorcyclists have to wear a protective helmet. If you are a male Sikh, you have to wear a turban, which means that you cannot wear a helmet. Some members of that community have successfully challenged the law, on the grounds that it prevented them from riding a motorcycle. Similarly, the law in the UK stipulates that animals should be stunned before being killed. But some Muslim and Jewish groups have successfully demanded exemption from that law, on the grounds that killing animals in that way goes against the commands of their religion. Advocates of special rights for minority groups are sympathetic to those demands, and quick to agree that the law so conceived does indeed breach freedom of religion for those groups and discriminates against their members.

The equality argument has elicited some criticisms. To begin with, as Okin has argued, it is insensitive to the subordinate place of women within most groups and to the importance, for those groups, of maintaining women in precisely such a place. As Okin notes, 'the sphere of personal, sexual, and reproductive life functions as a central focus of most cultures' (Okin, 1999, p. 13). In so far as women, much more than men, are at the heart of such a life, and in so far as most cultures seek to confer on men the power to control women, the latter are much more likely to be adversely affected by the defence and preservation of cultural practices. Okin uses a range of examples, from the founding myths of Greek antiquity, Christianity, and Judaism, as well as practices such as polygamy and clitoridectomy, in support of her claim that, in most cultures, women are seen as inferior to men, as sexually dangerous, and as wanton forces to be subdued and dominated. To allow groups to preserve their culture, Okin concludes, is at the same time to allow them to oppress women – in ways which are particularly worrisome for those liberals such as Kymlicka whose defence of minority rights is rooted in the value of equality. Against Okin, and in defence of minority rights, however, other feminists have argued that cultures are not as clearly patriarchal as Okin avers (Honig, 1999). True, they seek to control women's behaviour in general and sexuality in particular; at the same time, however, they also seek to control men's. Moreover, some cultural practices constrain women but at the same time grant them some freedoms. Take the case of the veil. It is standardly regarded by non-Muslims as a sign of the subjection of women. And in some cases, it might be. However, it can also be seen as a way for women to move in professional circles hitherto closed to them.

A second important criticism of the equality argument for minority rights has been articulated by Brian Barry in his influential *Culture and Equality* (Barry, 2001). On his view, equality does not justify religious exemptions from the law. Thus, Sikhs were not denied the opportunity to ride a motorcycle. Rather, their religion is such that they could not ride a motorcycle *and* be observant at the same time. Similarly, Jews and Muslims were not denied the opportunity to eat meat. Rather, their religion is such that they could not eat meat from animals killed as required by the law, and be observant at the same time. According to Barry, there is a difference between being denied an opportunity on religious grounds (as would be the case if the law said that the Sikhs cannot ride a motorcycle and that Jews and Muslims cannot eat meat) and not being able to avail oneself of existing opportunities. We all have to endure restrictions, in the light of our beliefs, on the choices that we make, and the case of religious minorities is no different. This is not to say that exemptions from rules can never be granted. On balance, there might be a good practical case, Barry concedes, for allowing the Sikhs not to wear a helmet (there are few of them, allowing them not to wear it would not be disruptive socially, etc.). In addition, there is a good, standardly liberal reason for allowing *everyone* not to wear a helmet – namely that the law is paternalistic, and, like all paternalistic restrictions, can be resisted by appealing to individual autonomy. (Obviously, this anti-paternalistic argument could not justify abolishing animal welfare laws.) But the important point, here, is that equality of opportunity as deployed through culture and community membership is not what does the justificatory work in support of granting exemptions from the law.

Barry's argument, note, crucially depends on a distinction between being denied an opportunity by the law and not being able to make a choice within the opportunities which it provides. However, this distinction might be thought problematic. In all likelihood, a Sikh who takes his religion seriously would say that he *cannot* ride a motorcycle. To be sure, he could travel by car. But the crucial point is that, from his point of view, the fact that it is his religion that prevents him from riding a motorcycle, and not the law directly, is irrelevant, precisely because we generally exercise little control over our religious beliefs. And this is why Kymlicka would retort against Barry that the state ought, on grounds of equality, to make provision for this particular individual.

Although egalitarian liberals sympathetic to minorities might be able to deal with Barry's challenge in the way just indicated, they face another, more serious problem. To the extent that they justify special rights by appealing to the value of individual autonomy, they will have difficulties accommodating minorities which reject that value. In that respect, as we will see below, they are sometimes charged by communitarians and some libertarians with not respecting cultural difference enough. The key issue, here, is that of toleration: to what extent can and must a liberal society tolerate illiberal cultures? The dilemma, for liberals such as Kymlicka, is this. On the one hand, they want to ensure equality between cultural groups and in particular between minority groups and the majority. On the other hand, they want to secure individual freedom and equality within groups. As a result, they will not be able to accede to the demands of *all* minorities: they will not allow a group not to send girls to school, for example. Nor will they allow for the circumcision of under-age girls, on the grounds that it deprives girls, and the women they later become, of the possibility of enjoying a fully flourishing sexual life.

In that respect, egalitarian liberalism is more protective of individual members of minorities than – paradoxically – the libertarian position we will examine in section 4. But it faces two difficulties. First, it faces difficulties with cases which do not involve such a radical loss of opportunity for minority members. Consider, for example, the case of headscarves in French schools. French law forbids children to wear religious clothing in state schools, on the grounds that the state is secular, and that state schools are the place where future citizens are being educated. Now, in some cases, Muslim girls are compelled by their family to wear a headscarf for religious and cultural reasons pertaining to (among other things) the importance of women's modesty for the preservation of the family's honour. In those cases, the headscarf is a sign of subjection, in the twofold sense that those girls are forced to wear it, and that it is a symbol of women's lower status within that culture. To be absolutely clear: I do not wish to imply that wearing the headscarf *always* has that meaning (nor do I wish to under-play the importance of the view that Western women are themselves subject to norms of beauty and sexual availability which are demeaning to them). All I mean is that, in some cases, wearing the headscarf does have that meaning, and these are the cases with which I am concerned here. The question, then, is whether an egalitarian liberal supportive of special minority rights can accede to those parents' demands that their daughters be exempt from the obligation not to wear religious clothing at school. Appealing to autonomy and equality to justify special rights might well deliver a framework of such rights which is far less respectful of minority cultures than their proponents are prepared to admit.

The second difficulty faced by Kymlicka's treatment of illiberal minorities is this. Imagine a minority which restricts the freedom of some of its members. At the bar of egalitarian justice, it lacks the right to do so. But does the majority have the right forcibly to impose on this group its own understanding of the importance of individual freedom? According to Kymlicka, it all depends on whether the illiberal minority is an immigrant group or a national minority, and on the kind of rights violations it commits. Thus, national minorities are free from interference by the majority, unless they are guilty of 'gross and systematic violations of human rights, such as slavery or genocide or mass torture and expulsions' (Kymlicka, 1995, p. 169). In cases where national minorities' illiberal practices fall short of gross human rights violations, all the liberal majority can do is speak out against them, and 'lend their support to any efforts the group makes to liberalize their culture' (ibid., p. 168). By contrast, it is not wrong 'for liberal states to insist that immigration entails accepting the legitimacy of state enforcement of liberal principles, so long as immigrants know this in advance, and none the less voluntarily choose to come' (ibid., p. 170). Notice, here again, that immigrant groups and national minorities are not treated in quite the same way.

Interestingly, Kymlicka's rationale for conferring on illiberal national minorities immunity from intervention on the part of the majority rests on the claim that, in the realm of international relations, states do not intervene in one another's affairs, except, precisely, in cases such as genocide and mass expulsions. According to Kymlicka, the reasons why one should be wary of intervening in another state's domestic policies also apply to national minorities: 'both foreign states and national minorities form distinct political communities, with their own claims to self-government. Attempts to impose liberal principles by force are often perceived, in both cases, as a form of aggression or paternalistic colonialism. And, as a result, these attempts often backfire' (1995, p. 167). Kymlicka may well have a point when pressing that reforms from the inside have a better chance of success at bringing about durable change than imposition from the outside. Nevertheless, his argument raises (at least) three questions. First, a staunch proponent of individual autonomy might well query his stand on non-intervention in those cases where the harm suffered by individual members is very severe indeed, even if it falls short of death or forced expulsion.

Second, it is not clear what his position commits him to regarding measures which, while not coercive of illiberal minorities, nevertheless substantially impinge on their internal practices. Imagine a national minority, for example, whose laws on marriage and divorce are generally detrimental to women – so that, for example, men can divorce without their spouse's consent whereas women cannot do so. The liberal state need not coerce this group into reforming its legal arrangements in order to preserve women's equal status. All it needs to do is decree that a woman from that group can obtain a divorce from her husband without the latter's consent. Although she would still be regarded as married in the eyes of the group, she would nevertheless be able to remarry under the state's law. This particular measure is not coercive; but it considerably weakens the force and bindingness of the group's legislation in ways which, since they facilitate exits from the group, might perhaps threaten its very fabric.

Third, and more widely, Kymlicka's defence of the principle of non-interference in national minorities' matters derives its strength from the analogous principle of non-interference in states' internal affairs. However, this principle might not be as strong as is sometimes suggested. In fact, humanitarian intervention might be warranted in a greater range of cases than Kymlicka seems to think.

To conclude, Kymlicka's defence of rights for cultural, ethnic, and religious minorities draws a sharp distinction between immigrants and national minorities. It is rooted in the liberal values of autonomy and equality, and seeks to limit groups' rights over their own individual members, precisely in the name of those two values. As we saw, it is on this last count that it is at its most vulnerable. In this, however, it is not alone: indeed, any broadly liberal theory of cultural accommodation which seeks, thus, to reconcile the rights of individuals with the rights of groups must deal with the problem of illiberal minorities. (For another example of such a theory, see Taylor, 1994.) Indeed, to the extent that liberals aim to show that liberal cultures must be willing to accommodate different cultures, this problem is perhaps the single most important issue which they should address. In what follows, we will examine how communitarianism and libertarianism deal with those issues.

3 Communitarianism and minorities

As we saw in chapter 1, communitarians criticize liberalism for overlooking the importance of community membership in the formation of individual identity, and insist that individuals cannot stand back from their community membership – widely defined – in the way liberals say they can. At first sight, it would seem as if the communitarian thinkers whose works we examined earlier, indeed communitarians in general, would have a lot to say about multiculturalism. And yet, accommodating the demands of cultural minorities is not as easy to communitarians as it seems.

Consider Michael Walzer's take on the issue in *Spheres of Justice* (Walzer, 1983, pp. 28ff.). In defining what a community is, he argues that the *political community* is where shared understandings are defined, as it is in such a community that history, culture, and language come together. However, as he himself notes, a political community may not always overlap with the historical communities over which it rules. Thus, Aborigines in Australia and Canada were living in those countries long before white settlers, whose descendants are now in power, got there. Whose shared meanings ought to prevail, then? According to Walzer, those of the political community override those of historical communities, because *politics* binds people together in a process of collective participation and decision-making. The problem, here, is that a group might refuse to be so bound by the larger political community of which it is part. If it claims, for example, a cultural exemption from a particular law, then the larger political community will violate that group's shared understandings by imposing that law on it. According to Walzer's own view – that we must respect all individuals as producers of social meanings, and that we must therefore respect the meanings they produce – the larger political community would in fact act wrongly.

Could Walzer concede the point, and say that, when there is a conflict between the larger political community and a cultural minority, the latter's social meanings should take precedence? Not really. For if justice is entirely bound up with *local* and culturally bounded social meanings, then it cannot adjudicate conflicts between different groups. This means, in turn, that it cannot adjudicate between different social meanings. Note that the point applies not merely to Walzer's theory, but to any view which says that justice is defined locally, and not universally. To put that point differently, on communitarian grounds, there is no *principled* argument which tells us *which* community matters most, and thus which community should see its own understanding of justice prevail. The only way to solve those conflicts is to resort to procedures such as majoritarian decision-making, which may well result in the oppression of minorities. It is unclear how a communitarian such as Walzer could accede to any of the four kinds of special claims which minority groups might want to make against the majority. In fact, in more recent work, Walzer has argued that the state should stand above its ethnic and national groups and remain neutral between them rather than support their particular way of life and culture (Walzer, 1994).

The sense in which a position on multiculturalism can be called 'communitarian' is this. Whereas egalitarian liberal proponents of group rights such as Kymlicka ground their theories in one or another overarching individualist value such as freedom or autonomy, the authors we are examining here implicitly or explicitly affirm that group membership is valuable irrespective of the extent to which it fosters individual freedom. Correlatively, conflicts between cultural minorities and the majority cannot be solved by appealing to universal principles, but on the contrary must be resolved through cultural dialogue. Nowhere are those two claims more in evidence than in Bikhu Parekh's recent *Rethinking Multiculturalism* (Parekh, 2000). According to Parekh – who would probably disagree with the label 'communitarian' but whose views are quite Walzerian in tone – individual autonomy is not the most important value of all. In fact, Parekh is at pains to stress that whatever universal principles there are can only be very general in content and scope, and must always be interpreted in the light of the cultural context in which they are meant to apply. Furthermore, human beings are deeply embedded in their culture, which provides them with the bedrock upon which they can lead what counts, for them, in that *milieu*, as flourishing lives. And it is for this reason, moreover, that human beings have obligations of loyalty and gratefulness to their cultural community. None of this implies that they are *determined* by their cultural environment, or that they ought never to criticize it. Rather, it suggests that it is appropriate for them to see themselves, and to insist that others see them, as culturally embedded beings.

Parekh's account of the importance of culture and its relationship to human nature cashes out into a fluid set of policies, including a constitutional framework of basic individual rights, a commitment to equality before the law, and the notion of collective rights. Parekh clearly affirms that not every cultural community warrants protection, and that not all cultural practice ought to be preserved (thus, he rules out female circumcision on under-age girls). At the same time, however, he insists that many do – and, indeed, many more, and in many more ways, than a number of egalitarian liberals would be prepared to accept. Thus – to give but one example – he argues that there are limits on freedom of speech, particularly when the latter is exercised in criticism of a religious group. Just as libel laws protect individuals from defamation, they ought also to protect cultural groups from defamation, provided that three conditions obtain: (a) those groups must be easily identifiable; (b) they must mean so much to their individual members that the latter would feel attacked personally if the group were attacked collectively; and (c) the group must be particularly vulnerable to discrimination (Parekh, 2000, ch. 10).

Egalitarian liberal advocates of group rights might be reluctant to confer such powers on the state in the name of culture. For even if it were possible to devise a 'libel test' as suggested by Parekh, they might argue that the resulting loss for individual freedom would be too great. Moreover, the first of Parekh's three conditions would worry them. For, contrary to what communitarians at times seem to suggest, cultural groups are not homogeneous. Thus, although a number of Muslims felt attacked, as Muslims, by Salman Rushdie's *The Satanic Verses*, many did not. Likewise, although a number of Catholics felt deeply offended, as Catholics, by Martin Scorsese's *The Last Temptation of Christ*, many welcomed, *as Catholics*, a movie which portrayed Jesus as a more human and fallible figure than that depicted by the Church's hierarchy. Moreover, many non-Muslims and non-Catholics found both works deeply challenging and interesting, and opposed attempts to censor them. To reiterate, the difficulty, for communitarians, or at least for those sympathetic to communitarianism's emphasis on the respect owed to individuals as embedded in their culture, is to identify *which* community matters, and *who* speaks for the community.

Incidentally, this point raises interesting issues for feminist critiques of minority rights. If, as Okin notes, groups are much more heterogeneous than advocates of group rights suggest, then this gives us a reason to heed the perspective on those groups not merely of outsiders, but of insiders as well. Thus, this gives us a reason to listen not only to Western liberal feminists' take on, say, veiling, early marriage, and polygamy, but also to feminist members of the groups in which those practices are common. On that view, one ought not to treat women as a single, homogeneous, category, but be aware of the many differences that there are between women members of any given cultural groups, and of the fact that some of them might be freely endorsing practices which others would regard as demeaning (Al-Hibri, 1999; Gilman, 1999; Post, 1999; Shachar, 2001).

4 A libertarian position: Kukathas's liberal archipelago

In the previous two sections, we examined some egalitarian liberal and communitarian arguments in favour of the protection of minority cultures. At first sight, it might seem that libertarians would have very little to say about this issue. For consider: libertarianism holds that *individuals* are the fundamental focus of our concern, that they only have rights not to be interfered with, and that they ought not to be coerced to live by principles which they do not endorse (provided that they respect other individuals' ownership rights). Accordingly, libertarians are unlikely to have much sympathy for the view that *groups* have rights against the majority, since group rights do not merely add to individual rights but can conflict with, indeed, undermine, them. Moreover, in so far as they reject positive rights to material help, they will reject the view that groups have special rights to financial subsidies for the purposes of preserving their culture. They might, however, have sympathy for individuals' demands to be exempted from obeying a given law on cultural grounds.

However, the most prominent account of multiculturalism by a libertarian, namely Chandran Kukathas's *The Liberal Archipelago*, suggests that a libertarian framework of individual rights may well end up conferring on cultural minority groups very extensive powers over their members – more extensive, in fact, than many communitarians (let alone liberals) would be happy to endorse (Kukathas, 2003). Before examining Kukathas's work in detail, a point of terminology is in order. Kukathas does not regard himself as a libertarian, and so to categorize him might, for that reason, prove controversial. Indeed, he does not at any point in his book explicitly endorse the two theses which mark out Nozickean libertarianism from other schools of thought, namely, self-ownership and the Lockean justification for private property. Having said that, there are good reasons, I believe, for attributing to him a set of views which Nozickean libertarians would find deeply congenial to their own. In particular, Kukathas repeatedly affirms that individuals should not be coerced to abide by principles in which they do not acquiesce. The role of the state, then, is merely to provide security, and to adjudicate conflicts between individuals and groups: it is not to enforce a particular conception of social justice, let alone to bring about equality. It is, in that sense, a minimal state, which is made up of a number of sub-associations with possibly great powers over their members, and to which only weak obligations are owed. To reiterate, no individual or group is under any duty to abide by the state's laws or arrangements if they do not consent to them, and thus no individual or group is under a duty to remain in that state.

At the root of Kukathas's theory is an account of human nature and human interests whereby the ability to live according to what one believes is right is the most important human motivation. What matters is not that individuals be able to choose, revise, and examine their ends (indeed, as he writes, 'the unexamined life may well be worth living' (2003, p. 59)) but that they do not have to live according to principles, beliefs, and norms which go against the dictates of their conscience. A free society, then, is one in which individuals enjoy freedom of conscience, which in turn requires that they enjoy freedom of association and its two corollaries, namely the freedom to exit whichever group(s) they belong to and a mutual toleration of associations, *be they liberal or illiberal*.

This last point is crucially important. For if individuals ought not to be coerced into living by norms and principles which they reject, then, by implication, they have the right to choose whether or not to associate with other like-minded individuals. And if they choose to associate with other individuals in groups which engage in illiberal, freedom-restrictive practices, then there is nothing which the wider society can do about it, *provided* that they retain the right to exit those groups. On that view, freedom of association and dissociation on the one hand enables cultural groups to retain considerable autonomy, and on the other hand enables individuals to retain their rights over themselves. According to Kukathas, his view does justice to the importance for individuals of belonging to cultural groups whose norms they endorse; at the same time, it remains sufficiently protective of individual freedom. Is he correct?

Let us look, first, at Kukathas's stand on the four kinds of special rights at issue in this chapter. As should be clear by now, Kukathas's liberal archipelago is not one in which cultural groups *as such* can claim special treatment from the state. For groups as such enjoy no special status; nor, in addition, do cultures. In fact, Kukathas explicitly notes, cultural difference is not an essential feature of human societies, but is entirely contingent on the kinds of associations which individuals are willing, at any time, to join. More strongly put, culture is not in any way fundamental to the constitution of group identity. To declare, then, that cultural groups have claims to special treatment against the state, both as groups and as cultural entities, is to confer on them a historical and normative importance which they lack. Moreover, cultural groups' insistence that they should receive such treatment as a matter of justice imposes on members of the majority the requirement to regard as important a set of values which they in fact reject. In that respect, it is incompatible with the requirement that all individuals enjoy freedom of conscience. Kukathas's treatment of language rights is instructive here. To be sure, he claims, individuals who belong to linguistic minorities should be free to use their own language when dealing with one another, or when educating their children. But they have no claim that the majority fund schooling in this particular language, simply because they cannot expect it to find this particular linguistic tradition worthwhile. Similarly, a group, as such, does not have a claim to special representation rights in the state's political institutions. For such a claim supposes that group identities are fixed, which they are not. Moreover, special representation rights are all too often justified by appeals to the importance of bringing about equality, be it equality between individuals or between groups, as well as of the importance of diversity. However, Kukathas notes, to confer special rights on minority groups will neither bring about equality nor do justice to the value of diversity. In fact, special representation is so controversial that it is likely to foster resentment of minorities, thus strengthening the oppressive, diversity-constraining culture in which they have to live. In addition, in so far as it is likely to work to the advantage of those who, within their minority culture, are already privileged, it will fail to promote the value of equality.

Kukathas, thus, advocates a policy of benign neglect, of the kind which Kymlicka, as we saw, strongly rejects, whereby minority groups are left to 'get on with it'. On his view, minority groups simply do not have a claim that the wider community help secure their survival as cultural entities.

Although minorities lack that claim, they have the right that the wider community not interfere in their internal arrangements. Of those two strands of Kukathas's account, the second – the claim that minorities should be free to organize their affairs as they see fit – has elicited the most attention, in so far as it allows for the existence of deeply illiberal communities. The first thing to note, though, is that it is linked to the issue of exemption rights for minority groups. For the very reason why groups should be left free to organize their affairs as they see fit – namely freedom of conscience – is also the reason why they must not force their members to stay, but instead must grant them the freedom to exit. As applied to the relationship between the wider community and the groups which constitute it, this suggests that, in some cases, the only way for the former to make it possible for the latter to exit from it is to grant its members exemptions from the law. Thus, in allowing Sikhs not to wear a helmet, the state makes it possible for them to live according to the dictates of their conscience, and at the same time to belong to the wider community. It is, in fact, a compromise solution, which offers what one may call (although Kukathas himself does not) a 'partial exit'. As Kukathas acknowledges, however, granting exemptions from the law will not always be possible. Should a minority group be denied it, it would either have to conform to the norms of the majority or, should that prove impossible (as against the dictates of its members' conscience), it would quite simply have to leave.

Setting the problem of exemption aside, it is time to address the most controversial aspect of Kukathas's liberal archipelago, namely its tolerance, in the name of freedom of conscience, of illiberal communities. As we saw, the only principle to which a free diverse society is bound is that of freedom of association, and its two corollaries, namely, freedom to exit and tolerance of all groups. It is important to remind ourselves, at this juncture, that, in requiring that individuals be left free to associate with whomever they wish, Kukathas is not insisting that they be able to make an informed choice. In fact, he stresses that most individuals do not even *choose* whether or not to belong to a particular group: they are born into it, and usually remain in it without questioning it. Still, what matters the most is that they be able to leave their group; and provided that their freedom to exit is protected, then the group can do whatever it wants.

I cannot, within the scope of this book, offer a comprehensive discussion of Kukathas's controversial claims. Instead, I will highlight two kinds of concern which a number of commentators have expressed. The first pertains to the freedom to exit itself. Individuals are free to leave, Kukathas notes, if their group does not coerce them to stay and if whatever arrangements it has in place to prevent them from leaving is denied validity by the wider community. The example of the law of marriage and divorce in Orthodox Judaism is a good example both of what Kukathas has in mind and of what many deem wrong with it. It is a law which is highly biased in favour of the husband and to the detriment of the wife. A man who wishes to get a divorce can get one without his wife's consent. By contrast, a woman who wishes to get a divorce needs her husband's consent – a consent which no rabbinical court can force him to give, however abusive he is towards her. In Kukathas's archipelago, the wider community is under no obligation whatsoever to recognize the validity of those marriages. In fact, it seems that it ought not to do so, since, in effect, this law coerces women, if their husbands refuse to let them go, to stay in an association (this particular marriage) in the terms of which they no longer acquiesce. In other words, the only way for a woman to leave her marriage would be to have the civil courts either grant her a divorce or refuse to recognize her marriage as valid, so that, although she would not be able to remarry under Orthodox Jewish law, she would be able legally to remarry under civil law.

But that, as a matter of fact, is a bone of contention between civil courts and some Orthodox Jewish communities. For the latter argue that, if the civil courts in effect override the rules of Orthodox Judaism, Orthodox Judaism will disappear. Whether that would happen is hard to tell. The important point, though, is this. It may be that the only way to guarantee individuals a substantial right to exit is for the wider society to intervene in the affairs of cultural minorities in such a way that the latter's survival would be under threat, as a result of which its members would no longer be able to live in a community whose norms they could, in conscience, abide by. And if that is correct, then it suggests that the libertarian take on multiculturalism as defended by Kukathas is, in fact, less congenial to freedom of conscience than it claims to be.

Moreover, some critics of Kukathas have argued that he takes insufficient account of the *costs* of exit. Imagine a religious minority whose members do not hold private property, as is the case, for example, with the Hutterites. Suppose that someone wants to leave the group. Unfortunately, because they own nothing in their own right, their decision to exit will leave them destitute, all the more so as they lack a right to assistance against the wider society (remember, we are in libertarian territory here). In what sense can we say that they are free to exit? Likewise, imagine someone who has been conditioned from childhood to believe that there is nothing worthwhile outside the group to which she belongs, and that the norms of that group – norms which afford her, as a woman, far fewer opportunities than they do men – are ones which she must endorse on pain of offending God. In what sense can we say that she is free to leave her group?

In the sense that neither of these two individuals are *coerced* to stay, Kukathas argues. In this, he implicitly invokes a particular conception of freedom, whereby it is enough for someone to be deemed free to do something, that he is not physically, and wilfully, interfered with by others. On that view, which Isaiah Berlin has memorably termed 'negative freedom', the costs of exiting from a group are irrelevant to the determination of that person as free (Berlin, 1969). Sceptics typically press two lines of argument against this conception of freedom and, by implication, Kukathas's application of it in his treatment of illiberal minorities. First, some argue that negative freedom is an impoverished conception of freedom, which has counter-intuitive implications (for example, a slave whose master never interferes with him nevertheless is free (Pettit, 1997)) and fails adequately to distinguish between meaningful and meaningless freedoms (Taylor, 1979b). Second, others claim that, even if it is enough for someone to be free that he is not interfered with by others, one must take into account the worth of that freedom (Rawls, 1999a). On this view, if one lacks the material resources and/or personal abilities to act, one may well be free, but one's freedom will be worthless. By implication, then, the freedom to exit one's community is worthless if one lacks the resources or the personal capacities to do so, as would be the case with, respectively, the Hutterites and the woman who has been conditioned since childhood to abide by the norms of her group.

So far, I have mentioned some concerns which critics of Kukathas have raised regarding his account of the freedom to exit. The other concern pertains to the extent to which the wider community ought to allow cultural minorities free rein in their internal affairs. As we have seen, Kukathas insists that minorities ought not to be interfered with if they grant their members the freedom to exit. Moreover, he believes that the freedom to exit is nothing more than the ability to leave without interference. But this – some critics have argued – can apply only to adult and mentally competent group members, and not to children or weak and vulnerable adults. Take the case of children. Unlike competent adults in full possession of their capacities, children are subject to their parents' authority, and cannot really be regarded as free to leave their group. And yet Kukathas himself acknowledges that, in his liberal archipelago, communities would be allowed not to educate their children, to deny them life-saving medical treatment, to inflict on them severe corporal punishment, indeed, to treat them in ways which, in the wider society, would be regarded as a form of abuse, not to say torture. They would also be allowed to inflict harm on their vulnerable members, such as the mentally ill, for example, or the physically weak, or the powerless.

The challenge which Kukathas faces is this. If parents' claim to treat their children in those ways derives not from the importance of *cultural* membership, but from the importance of respecting their desire not to live by norms which they do not endorse, then there does not seem to be any reason to disallow them from scaring and maiming their children simply because they wish to do so. Nor, in fact, does there seem to be any reason to disallow them from killing their children. And nor is there any reason to punish powerful group members for abusing those weaker than they are – for example, to punish men for beating up their wives as allowed by their religion (Barry, 2001). Kukathas is keen to rebut the charge that his theory of toleration has those perverse consequences. When a group is known to condone clearly oppressive practices, he claims, the established authorities do lack the right to intervene by force, but should try persuasion instead, since conversion through persuasion is more likely to work. Moreover, it is also important to realize that individuals are bound by the norms of the wider society in which they live, such as norms which dictate against, for example, mutilating children at will, and are likely to feel under pressure to conform to those norms. And if that does not happen, as Kukathas acknowledges that it might not, then we should still resist the temptation of entrusting the established authorities to step in. All we can say is that the role of the state is merely to keep the peace.

Sceptics are unlikely to be convinced. They will argue that Kukathas's argument implies that, so long as a practice, be it cultural or not, does not threaten the peace, then the state ought not to interfere with it, however oppressive it is to those on the receiving end of it (provided that it falls short of outright coercion), and however harmful it is to vulnerable group members. And there are two reasons why sceptics might want to reject that. On Kukathas's own terms, they might be tempted to insist, unbridled toleration results in groups and parents being allowed to treat children and vulnerable adults in such a way that they might never develop into, or be, the kind of adults for whom that freedom makes sense. As a result, it fails to make good on its promise to ensure that all individuals live by the dictates of their conscience. True, they might concede to Kukathas, those children and vulnerable adults will enjoy freedom of conscience, in Kukathas's archipelago, to the extent that they can live according to their beliefs. And if those beliefs have been instilled in them by a conditioning made of years of constant abuse, or are impressed on them, in adult-hood, by the conforming mechanism of constant fear, then so be it. But the sceptics will wonder to what extent one can still say that those individuals live according to the dictates of their *conscience*, rather than to those of the more powerful. Second, sceptics will argue, if that is what freedom of conscience requires – the toleration of severely illib-eral communities, and thereby of harmful and abusive practices towards the vulnerable – then it exacts too high a price, and should be curbed, for the sake of protecting other fundamental interests of human beings.

To this, Kukathas replies that we should never lose sight of the fact that states too are oppressive – far more so, in fact, than most cultural groups. Nor should we deceive ourselves in thinking that we can articulate a conception of human interests, above and beyond the interest in freedom of conscience, which is uncontroversial enough that it can be imposed on all of us without abuse of power. Whether or not his argument can convince anyone but the staunchest opponents of state intervention in people's lives remains to be seen.

5 Conclusion

All major schools of thought face difficulties when dealing with the question of the ways in which the cultural majority should deal with minorities. Notwithstanding their professed belief in the importance of communal attachments, communitarians will have trouble accom-modating the demands of minorities so long as they cannot tell us whose values should prevail. Those libertarians who hope to do justice to the importance of communal membership solely by appealing to individual rights have to deal with the objection that they cannot in fact do so. As to egalitarian liberals who, unlike libertarians, are willing to grant group rights to communities themselves, they nevertheless also face difficulties in reconciling individual rights with group rights.

4 National Self-Determination

1 Introduction

In the previous chapter, we examined a number of arguments for, and against, conferring special rights on ethnic, cultural, and religious minorities. In the next two chapters, we will assess liberal, communitarian, and libertarian accounts of the principles under which a politically sovereign community ought to behave towards similar communities, as well as towards individual foreigners. In this chapter, we will look at the conditions under which a national community which is not yet a nation-state is entitled to become one. Conversely, we will look at what a sovereign nation-state owes to national communities which aspire to statehood. Our topic here, thus, is the principle of national self-determination, whereby 'the political and national units should be congruent' (Gellner, 1983, p. 55).

Judging by recent facts, the principle, which came to life in Europe in the middle of the nineteenth century, is enjoying a strong political resurgence. In 1989, as powerful democratic movements toppled communist regimes in Eastern Europe, the land mass to the east of Poland and the north of China was still within the jurisdiction of a single, multinational state, the USSR. In December 1991, the USSR was broken up into a number of sovereign republics along ethnic lines. Between 1992 and 2006, Yugoslavia, which had been a multinational state since 1918, progressively fell apart and gave rise to several independent states, such as Croatia and Bosnia-Herzegovina, again along largely ethnic lines. Likewise, Slovakia and the Czech Republic, which had formed one country since the end of the First World War, became independent from one another in 1993. In the UK, the National Scottish Party has been at the forefront of Scottish demands for independence. Further to the west still, a number of Québécois are pressing for secession from Canada.

Our focus in this chapter, then, is on the justifications which, according to liberals, communitarians, and libertarians, support national groups' demands for statehood. As we will see, the literature on national self-determination is dominated by philosophers of a liberal bent; as we will also see, it is in this area, perhaps more than in the field of multiculturalism, that liberal philosophers have made the greatest efforts to accommodate some of the communitarian views which we highlighted in chapter 1. Before we proceed, however, we will have to bear in mind the following points.

First, *national* self-determination is only one instantiation of the more general demand for *political* self-determination. While the former stipulates that a nation should determine its own future, the latter makes no reference to the national identity of the community's members. Accordingly, a claim for political self-determination can (conceptually) be made by individuals of different national identities who nevertheless perceive themselves to constitute a political community – albeit not a national one. A claim for national self-determination cannot. In this chapter, I will focus on national self-determination, because it has far more political appeal, and is thus far more prevalent, than claims for political self-determination.

Second, we will need a working definition of *nations, national identity*, and *nationalism*. The literature generated by those issues is so voluminous, particularly when it comes to definitions, that we cannot hope to get to grips with its details here. For our purposes, however, David Miller's definition of a nation is particularly helpful. A nation, he writes, is a 'community (1) constituted by shared belief and mutual commitment, (2) extended in history, (3) active in character, (4) connected to a particular territory, and (5) marked off from other communities by its distinct public culture' (Miller, 1995, p. 27). In Benedict Anderson's well-known words, a nation is also an 'imagined community', since its members do not know one another personally, and have very little contact with one another (Anderson, 1991). What makes a public culture *national* is, of course, a difficult issue, but elements such as the use of distinct myths, symbols, practices, and language, which unite individuals of different social and economic backgrounds and differentiate them from other individuals, matter crucially. Thus, the use of the French language is not enough, on its own, to differentiate a French person from a French *Canadian* person. Take, by contrast, the commemoration of the storming of the Bastille prison on 14 July 1789, the capacity and willingness to talk endlessly about food, a strong attachment to the cycling race the Tour de France, and a propensity to manifest political discontent by going on strike or taking to the streets at the drop of a hat. Those features together are enough to confer on the community of diverse individuals living within the borders of what is known as France a national character which is different from that of the French Canadian community.

Third, the relationship between nation and state which the principle of national self-determination is meant to capture is bidirectional. Looking from the nation to the state, it is argued that a national community has a claim to govern itself without interference from other national communities, as a fully sovereign body. Looking from the state to the nation, it is also argued by some proponents of national self-determination that a state fulfils its tasks best if the unit over which it exercises sovereignty is a nation.

Fourth, we will need to distinguish between two kinds of self-determination claim. On the one hand, a national community might wish to make a claim against another such community with which it stands in a relationship of political and juridical inequality. On the other hand, a national community might wish to secede from a community with which it stands in a relationship of political and juridical equality and forms a multinational, typically federal, community. Palestinian claims to national self-determination against Israel are an example of the former, in so far as Palestinians are not equal partners with Israel in an Israeli–Palestinian state. By contrast, claims such as made by French Canadian nationalists in Quebec against the rest of Canada illustrate the latter, in so far as the inhabitants of Quebec are no less citizens, in the federal, multinational state of Canada, than citizens from Manitoba or British Columbia. This factual difference between non-secessionist and secessionist claims for national self-determination is morally relevant in the following ways. For a start, claims for secession are not coterminous with claims for national self-determination: a secessionist demand might well succeed for reasons which have nothing to do with the desire, on the part of the seceding group, to govern itself along national lines, but everything to do with, for example, what it perceives as excessive economic demands on the part of the larger community. Moreover (or so some may argue), in cases of secession, more so than in cases of what some have called national liberation, the consequences of separation for the group from which it is sought ought to be taken on board. In other words, the particular relationship that exists between the secessionist group and the group from which it wants to secede is such that, even if one can make a case for the right to national self-determination in general, one cannot straightforwardly infer that this national group has the right to secede. Throughout this chapter, then, we will examine both kinds of claim through the lenses of our three schools of thought.

Fifth, we will also need to keep sight of the territorial dimension of national self-determination. This is because a national community which wishes to become a sovereign, independent state is thereby claiming the right to exercise jurisdiction over a territory. In so doing, it is seeking to remove this territory, and its natural resources, from the jurisdiction of other states. This, in turn, means that its demand for self-determination imposes material costs on other national communities which they might not be willing or able to bear. Accordingly, a national community which demands that other, similar communities not interfere in its internal affairs will not have done enough to establish its claim – should it make any – to conduct its affairs over this, rather than that, territory. Thus, even if Palestinians can make a successful claim to statehood, they will not have thereby shown that they ought to be able to form their state in Gaza, the West Bank, and East Jerusalem, rather than, for example, in inhabited territories in which no other country has an interest.

2 Liberal nationalism

2.1 Self-determination claims

It might seem, at first sight, that liberalism and nationalism cannot happily coexist. For liberalism is standardly thought to imply a commitment to reason, as well as adherence to universal principles which are justified by appealing to facts about human beings irrespective of their communal belonging. Nationalism, by contrast, is often taken to imply an irrational attachment to one's national community, contempt for all things different, and reliance on emotions rather than reason. Or so the caricatural accounts of liberalism and nationalism would have us believe. However, from the late 1980s onwards, a number of philosophers have articulated and defended what is now known as 'liberal nationalism'. According to liberal nationalism, claims to national self-determination, far from being at odds with liberalism, are in fact supported by it. Interestingly, there is a sense in which liberal nationalism is a syncretion of liberalism and communitarianism. As we saw in chapter 1, communitarians charge Rawlsian liberals for not being sufficiently attentive to the importance of communal attachments for the formation of the self. As we also saw in chapter 3, multiculturalist liberals such as Kymlicka have taken that point on board and used it as the basis for their defence of minority rights. Liberal nationalism straightforwardly pursues this line of thought and argues that national belonging is, for the overwhelming majority of individuals, a crucial component of their identity.

Note, though, that, for those liberals, national identity is to be understood in a cultural, rather than an ethnic, sense. To be sure, nationality and ethnicity do overlap. However, as multi-ethnic nations show, they are not identical: thus, Americans form a nation, whether they are black, Jewish, Latino, or Irish. The question is whether ethnicity *should* mark off self-determining communities from one another. And, to this question, the liberal nationalist answer is, unambiguously, a 'no'. For it is central to liberalism – or at least to *contemporary* liberalism – first, that, at least up to a point, individuals should not be disadvantaged for reasons which are beyond their control, and, second (and relatedly), that they be seen and treated as authors of their own lives. If so, then to use ethnicity, over which we clearly have no control, as the basis for national self-determination claims is clearly illiberal (Gans, 2003; Miller, 1995; Tamir, 1993).

Let us look a bit more closely at the standard liberal nationalist defence of the view that nations need their own states. With nuances and qualifications which need not detain us here, it can be formalized as follows (Miller, 1995; Margalit and Raz, 1990; Tamir, 1993).

1 Individuals have a fundamental right to live in an environment which is conducive to their well-being.
2 National identity is a constitutive element of individual well-being. Therefore,
3 Individuals have a fundamental right to the preservation of their national identity. Furthermore,
4 National identity is best preserved by political arrangements which enable individuals to shape the national life of their community. Therefore,
5 Individuals have a right to national self-determination.

This argument is liberal in the following respects. First, as claim (2) suggests, it speaks of the importance of national identity for *individuals*, and does not ascribe interests to groups as such, independently of the interests of their members. Put differently, individuals, and not groups, are the fundamental units of moral and political discourse.

Second, and relatedly, most of its proponents (with the notable exception of Miller) couch national self-determination claims in the language of rights – a hallmark of liberalism. Whether or not the right is held by individuals or groups is one of the points of debate among liberal nationalists. As we saw in chapter 2, the most prominent theories of rights are, respectively, the choice-based theory and the interest-based theory. Liberal nationalists subscribe to the latter, according to which, you recall, for A to have a right that B do or do not P, means that an interest of A's is strong enough to warrant holding B under a duty to do, or not do, P. The question, then, is whether this definition can apply to groups – whether, that is, there can be collective, rather than individual, rights. As some rights theorists have argued, for a right to be collective, it must protect a *communal* good, namely a good which has worth to individuals *qua* members of a group whose good it is, and not *qua* human beings (P. Jones, 1999; Waldron, 1993).

National self-determination is a paradigmatic example of a communal good. Suppose that my nation is recognized as a state by the international community and that elections are being organized for the first time. That is of value to me, for example because it enables me to have a say in the way the social and political environment in which I live is shaped. But it is only *qua* member of that community that I can find this project worthwhile. If I had to live in a different country to the one where I was born and brought up, and if I did not identify with that country, the right to political participation would not have the same value to me.

Thus, national self-determination is an example of a good which is jointly valuable and whose worth can only be understood as the worth it has to individuals *qua* members of a national group. However, in so far as the rights which protect such goods are grounded in the importance of those goods for individuals, and not for groups themselves, they stand firmly in the liberal tradition.

Liberal nationalist arguments for national self-determination, thus, are liberal in that they protect individuals' fundamental interest in furthering their well-being, of which national identity (or so those arguments tell us) is a constitutive element. Moreover, and by implication, liberal nationalists impose legitimacy conditions on the kind of claims which national communities are allowed to make when demanding the right to determine their own future. Thus, a nation which, once granted sovereignty over its own affairs, would violate the rights of its individual members lacks a claim to do so. We touched on this issue briefly in chapter 3, when examining Will Kymlicka's defence of special rights for national minorities. Kymlicka, you recall, grants national minorities the right to conduct illiberal policies which fall short of gross human rights violations, on the grounds that those minorities should not be more liable to outside intervention than states are. For consistency's sake, then, he should be as 'liberal' with national minorities' claims for national self-determination. By contrast, some liberal nationalists might perhaps want to offer a more restrictive account of the principles by which national communities which aspire to sovereignty ought to treat their individual members. Be that as it may – and, as we will see, in contrast with both communitarians and libertarians – liberal nationalists are not willing to grant sovereignty to any national group which is demanding it, precisely because they justify national self-determination by appealing to the importance of furthering individual well-being.

Before reviewing some critical comments on the liberal nationalist argument, it is worth examining its applicability to the case of secession. As I suggested above, the claim that a national community has a *prima facie* right to determine its own future does not suffice to show that it has a right to secede from another group. To reiterate, the particular relationship that exists between the secessionist group and the community from which it wants to secede is one of political and juridical equality. As a result, the detrimental consequences of secession on the latter ought to be taken into account. By contrast, a dominant, colonial power has much less of a claim, if any claim at all, to have its interests taken into account by the national communities it has oppressed. With that proviso in place, liberal nationalists should have no difficulty applying their defence of national self-determination in general to secession in particular.

So much, then, for describing that defence. What are we to make of it? Claim (1), which states that individuals have a fundamental right to live in an environment which is conducive to their well-being, seems straightforwardly true. Claim (2), which states that national identity is a constitutive element of individual well-being, is more problematic. For a start, it is not true of everybody that membership in a nation furthers their well-being. In some cases, it adversely affects them, for example when the values and beliefs of that nation run counter to their deeply held convictions, wishes, and plans of life. Consider, for example, a non-Catholic Irish woman burdened by an unwanted pregnancy. It is not clear that her well-being is served by her membership in a national community which regards adherence to Roman Catholicism, and thereby the condemnation of abortion, as a central component of its identity. Moreover, some forms of national identity are morally obnoxious. It is equally unclear, for example, in what sense membership in a national community of white supremacists which has succeeded in expelling all non-white people contributes to those white individuals' well-being (Caney, 1996).

In addition, some forms of national identity are formed through manipulation and collective lies. The French, for example, see their nation as a standard-bearer for universal human rights. It is, by and large, a myth, which was created and sustained, over two centuries, through the systematic distortion of French history in history curricula and public discourses. Some liberal nationalists are relatively sanguine about the pervasiveness, indeed, the necessity, of such myths (Miller, 1995). Other liberals might cast doubt, though, on the connection between individual well-being and national identity so constructed. Finally, as we saw in chapter 3, other forms of identities than ones bound with localities (be they local, or national, or supranational) are crucially important to individuals – such as cultural and/or religious identities. Indeed some kinds of identity, such as Roman Catholicism, transcend borders. The question, then, is why national identities should be privileged over others.

Let us assume, for the sake of argument, that the liberal nationalist defence of national self-determination can meet those various objections. It would still have to show that the preservation of national identity is important enough to justify granting full sovereignty to national communities. A number of commentators have expressed scepticism on that particular point, and have indicated that other institutional arrangements falling short of full sovereignty might well do the job properly. Thus, Allen Buchanan argues that national minorities could be granted self-government rights within multinational, federal states, including special property rights over the territory over which they wish to govern, special rights to restrict entry into their community, special language rights, and so on (Buchanan, 1991, 2004).

The provisions which he recommends are of the kind we examined in chapter 3, and I will not revisit them here. It is worth pointing out, however, that his critique of the argument for national self-determination as grounded in cultural preservation leads him to endorse a very restrictive justification for secession in particular, and national self-determination in general. On his view, only when a national group is threatened with cultural *extinction* or with literal genocide, or when it has been the victim of severe rights violations, can it make a claim for full sovereignty. To many, those conditions seem unduly demanding. Why should a national group have a right to secede *only* if its survival is at stake, or if it has been the victim of injustice? Imagine two such groups, S and T, where S wants to secede from T. T refuses, on the grounds that S could survive as a national group within T, and/or that S has not been seriously victimized by T. S could legitimately reply, perhaps, that the members of T who do not share S's national identity have the opportunity to live in a fully self-determining community along national lines. So why, S's members might ask, should they be denied that opportunity? A national group which is already enjoying the privilege of self-government can hardly refuse that privilege to another national group on the grounds that national identity should not be isolated as particularly important when deciding who should govern whom. Thus, to more generous advocates of national self-determination in general and secession in particular, the commission of serious injustice by T on S, or the fact that S risks extinction, cannot be *necessary* conditions for the legitimacy of S's aspiration to full sovereignty (Patten, 2002).

So far, we have examined liberal nationalist claims in support of the view that nations need states. Interestingly, some liberal nationalists have argued that states also need nations. One prominent argument to that effect, which points to the connections between the values of justice and national self-determination, has been put forward by David Miller. In a nutshell, Miller argues that the business of the state is (among other things) to legitimize and implement principles of justice, and that it will do its job better, on both counts, if it governs a relatively homogeneous and unified nation, whose members agree that they are tied by bonds of solidarity (Miller, 1995). Whatever the merits of Miller's argument, it is a pragmatic defence of national self-determination – one which appeals to the practical value of national identity for justice, rather than to its value for individual well-being.

To conclude, liberal nationalist justifications for national self-determination appeal to the importance, for individuals, of national belonging, and, for the state, of the nation. As we noted at the outset, it is sympathetic to standard communitarian criticisms of contemporary liberalism. But as we will see in section 3, it differs from communitarian accounts of national self-determination in some important respects. Beforehand, however, let us turn to liberal nationalist justifications for territorial claims.

2.2 Territorial claims
The right to exercise sovereignty over a piece of territory is distinct from the right to exercise collective government. The latter is a right not to be interfered with by other political communities in the conduct

of domestic policies. The former is a right to conduct domestic poli-cies in a specific geographical area. Put differently, territorial rights pertain to the location of collective government. By granting such rights to a given political community, one removes the territory in question from the jurisdiction of another political community, which itself may have a strong interest in not relinquishing it. For this reason, territorial rights require a separate justification (Gans, 2003).

The most prevalent liberal nationalist argument for such rights appeals to the importance of the territory to which a national com-munity lays claim for the latter's culture (Meisels, 2005; Moore, 2001). On this view, if there is a strong connection between a particular ter-ritory and a national community, the latter has a *prima facie* right to exercise jurisdiction over it. A cursory look at the academic literature on the topic, as well as current territorial disputes, suggests that there are two main reasons why a national community will attach particu-lar importance to a given territory. First, some national communities argue that a particular land is theirs in so far as it is their cultural bedrock – the nation's cradle, as it were, the place where events deci-sive to the nation's identity took place. Zionist claims to sovereignty over the land of Israel are a paradigmatic example of this view. Second, some national communities argue that, having lived and settled con-tinuously on a particular territory, they have shaped and enriched it in such ways that the territory has become the expression of their national culture. Thus, over time, the territory has ceased to be a mere piece of land: it is, rather, a tapestry of buildings, landscapes, and modes of living, which is distinct from territories on which other national communities have also settled.

Now, liberal nationalists argue that national identity is a constitu-tive element of individual well-being, and that individuals have a fun-damental right to the preservation of their national identity. On that view, it seems to follow, quite naturally, that a self-determining national community should be granted sovereignty over the territory which is central to its cultural identity in the ways just described. However, this particular justification for territorial rights will not work in those cases where two or more national communities make a similar claim to exercise sovereignty over the same territory. Again, the Israeli–Palestinian conflict is a case in point. Both Israelis and Palestinians invest this particular piece of land with enormous cul-tural and symbolic significance. Both aver that this land is *their* land, as Jews and Palestinians, precisely in so far as it is their nation's cradle, and/or as they have settled on, and shaped, the land in the ways just described. Both, admittedly, have a point. It is therefore quite hard to discern the applicability of the liberal nationalist argument for territorial rights to cases such as these, where a resolution of the conflict is most urgently needed.

3 Communitarianism and national self-determination

3.1 Self-determination claims

Just as liberalism seems, at first sight, obviously unfriendly to nationalist claims, communitarianism appears, again at first sight, obviously sympathetic to them. National identity provides the basis for the kind of social connectedness which, communitarians insist, is essential to the pursuit of the common good. The question, then, is whether there can be a communitarian justification for national self-determination which substantially differs from the liberal nationalist account. And it seems that there can be. Such a justification would have to appeal to the importance of national identity, of course; but it would also have to stress that it is relatively fixed, or at any rate far less a matter of choice and critical reflection than liberal nationalists such as Miller and Tamir seem to allow. In Charles Taylor's words,

> I may come to realize that belonging to a given culture is part of my identity, because outside of the reference points of *this* culture I could not begin to put to myself, let alone answer, those questions of ultimate significance that are peculiarly in the repertoire of the human subject. Outside *this* culture, I would not know who I was as a human subject. So *this* culture helps to identify me . . . Since the Romantic insight is that we need a language in the broadest sense in order to discover our humanity, and that this language is something we have access to through our community, it is natural that the community defined by natural language should become one of the most important poles of identification for the civilization that is heir to the Romantics. (Taylor, 1993, pp. 45–6; emphases added)

The foregoing points apply to both 'directions' of the principle of national self-determination. Let us initially look at the first prong of the principle through communitarian lenses. The principle, in order to be distinctively communitarian, would have to point to the importance of national identity for promoting a conception of the good life through the state. Thus, one sometimes hears the view that to be Greek means to belong to the Greek Orthodox Church, and that to belong to the Greek Orthodox Church is central to any conception of the good life, so that Greek national identity is inextricably linked, on that account, to this particular conception of the good, both at the individual and the collective level (Kymlicka, 2001, p. 265).

So much, then, for the view that nations need their states. As for the claim that states ought to be nations, it too can find support in communitarian theory. As we saw in chapter 1, communitarians charge Rawlsian liberalism for offering a very impoverished conception of the relationship that ties the individual to his or her community. In particular, they argue, there is something inherently valuable in individuals' participating in the political institutions of their state with a view to articulating, and implementing, a conception of the common good. It is easy to discern how some communitarian advocates of national self-determination could press that citizens are more likely to find the motivation necessary to sustain that level of political engagement if they are bound to one another by the cultural, historical, and linguistic ties of common nationality.

Clearly, then, communitarian understandings of national self-determination impose different demands on group members than liberal accounts of it. On the one hand, communitarianism, unlike liberalism, does not have to rule out, from the outset, the possibility that national identity can be conceived of along ethnic, rather than cultural, lines. By downplaying the importance of individual choice between, and critical distancing from, sources of allegiance, they are in a position to allow that individuals may identify with, say, the French nation, not as a community which celebrates the storming of the Bastille and likes going on strike, but as a community of white, French-speaking descendants of the Gauls. On that view, the fact that France has never been such a community is neither here nor there.

On the other hand, communitarianism will look with far greater sympathy than liberals (even, I surmise, liberal nationalists) will on policies which will aim at instilling in citizens a very strong sense of identification with their nation, at the cost of some of their rights. For example, they might resist demands for special linguistic rights, on the grounds that the dominant language is the most important medium through which the national culture is shaped and articulated, and that any newcomer must learn it and be able fully to function in it. Or they might advocate a compulsory and short-term civil service. In Daniel Bell's words, such a scheme 'will strengthen the moral bonds holding the nation together and thus narrow the gap between citizens' latent attachments to their nation and how they manifest these feelings in practice' (Bell, 1993, p. 141).

Finally, were communitarians tempted to articulate their defence of national self-determination in the language of rights, they – or at least the most radical among them – would be more friendly to what Peter Jones has called corporate, rather than collective, rights (P. Jones, 1999; Van Dyke, 1995). As we saw at the beginning of section 2, collective rights protect communal goods, which have value to individuals *qua* group members, and not *qua* human beings. Accordingly, those rights are held by individuals taken together as group members. By contrast, corporate rights are held by a group as such and not held jointly by its members. They suppose that the moral standing of a group is not reducible to the moral standing of the group's members. Liberals, affirming as they do that individuals, and not groups, are the primary units of moral concern, cannot endorse corporate rights. Communitarians, by contrast, can.

It would be tempting to assume that communitarians are necessarily sympathetic to the value of national self-determination. In fact, some of the most prominent communitarian thinkers, namely Michael Sandel and Alasdair McIntyre, have expressed scepticism towards the view that national and political boundaries must be coterminous. As Sandel writes, 'By the mid- or late twentieth century, the national republic had run its course. Except for extraordinary moments, such as war, the nation proved too vast a scale across which to cultivate the shared self-understandings necessary to community in the formative, or constitutive sense' (Sandel, 1984, p. 93). And revealingly, when listing communal sources of identity, McIntyre mentions 'the family, the neighbourhood, the city and the tribe', but not the nation (McIntyre, 1981, p. 221).

It is easy to see, in fact, why (some) communitarians resist the appeal of the nation-state. The nation, you recall, is an imagined community whose members do not know each other personally. Some communitarians doubt that fellow nationals can have with one another the ties which would provide them with a genuine sense of belonging. Moreover, to the extent that, as we saw in chapter 1, communitarians extol the virtues of participating in public institutions so as to further the common good, they are less likely to find much of value, on that score, in the distanced, anonymous, large-scale political institutions of the nation-state.

In addition, as we also saw in chapter 3, and to echo a point made at the end of section 2 above, it is not inherent in the communitarian enterprise that it should be committed to preserving a particular kind of community, rather than another. In other words, it is not committed to the view that national belonging is a more meaningful source of identity than other kinds of communal belonging. As Charles Taylor himself points out in his writings on Québécois separatism, to claim that communal belonging matters is one thing; to identify which communal belonging matters requires a separate argument (Taylor, 1993).

Finally, and as we also saw in chapter 1, a recurrent theme of the communitarian critique of contemporary liberalism is the latter's excessive reliance (in communitarian eyes) on rights discourse. If we were united as a community, and if we had a shared understanding of the values we want to pursue and the ways we want to treat each other, rights would not be necessary. Instead, communitarians such as Sandel argue, we should aim at bringing about a world in which we will not need to invoke our rights against others. As applied to the issue at hand, this criticism is particularly salient. For just as scepticism towards rights is prevalent in communitarian thinking, worries about the implications of granting rights to national self-determination to national communities is a common trope of studies of nationalism. The worry is that, by granting national self-determination on a large scale as a matter of right, we open the door for the breaking-up of many a political community, against the wishes of majorities whose understanding of the common good revolves, precisely, around the value of coexisting nationalities (Beiner, 1998).

To conclude, and in keeping with the conclusions we reached in chapter 3 when discussing communitarian views on minority rights, it is hard to discern a coherent and unified communitarian position on national self-determination – for the simple and often mentioned reason that communitarians are not inherently committed to attaching value to a particular kind of community rather than to another.

3.2 Territorial claims

Communitarian philosophers have not spent much time on the issue of territorial disputes. From our construal of communitarian positions on national self-determination, we can assume that someone of a strong communitarian bent might be tempted to accept the liberal nationalist argument for territorial rights as outlined in section 2.2. But they might also want to push it further, and claim that a national community *cannot* be itself, and remain itself, unless it is granted full sovereignty over the land that constitutes its cradle, or the land which it has shaped over the centuries. On that view, the nation currently called France would cease to exist as France if its entire population were to leave the territory currently known as France and to occupy Southern Australia. On the other hand, of course, communitarians might prefer to align themselves with Sandel and McIntyre's scepticism about the nation-state, and might thus reject the claim that *national* communities are linked to particular territories in the ways suggested above. In other words, there does not seem to be a distinctive communitarian position on the ethical issues raised by the location of national, self-determining communities.

4 Libertarianism and national self-determination

4.1 Self-determination claims

Whereas liberalism and communitarianism endorse national self-determination as a valuable ideal, libertarianism does not. More precisely, libertarians cannot accept that national identity matters crucially to individuals' well-being and, therefore, that national communities should enjoy political sovereignty. Nor can it endorse the claim that states *ought* to be nations, for the simple reason that states have only minimal functions (in essence, ensuring that individuals respect one another's fundamental civil and political rights), for which the common ties of nationality are not necessary.

At the heart of the libertarian stand on national self-determination lies the view that groups, and their identities, are in constant flux, so that one cannot coherently identify groups, and therefore assign rights to them *a priori*. More specifically to the issue at hand, nations themselves are in flux, so that we cannot identify a nation and then grant it the right to determine its own future. Moreover, we cannot assume that national belonging matters to all individuals. Rather, in order to decide to whom rights of self-determination *tout court* should be granted, we must look to individuals' cultural attachments and self-perception. We must, in other words, ask them to which group they regard themselves as belonging, and whether or not they acknowledge the authority of those who are calling for self-determination on their behalf. On that view, provided that a group would not unjustly harm other groups by determining its own future, the consent of its members to self-determination is sufficient to render their claim to self-determination legitimate (Beran, 1984; Kukathas, 2003; Philpott, 1995; Wellman, 1995).

This clearly is not an argument in favour of *national* self-determination. To be sure, if a group of individuals attach importance to their national identity and believe that it will be best preserved through statehood, then, provided that they would not unjustly harm others in so doing, their claim to national self-determination is valid. But the fact that theirs is a claim to national self-determination is entirely contingent on the fact that they happen to regard their national identity as that which deserves the protection of an independent and sovereign state. Were they to believe, instead, that their racial identity, or their religion, is central to their identity, or were they merely to express the wish to live together, they could make an equally valid claim to self-determination.

What gives this argument a libertarian flavour is its reliance on individuals' consent as a sufficient condition (together with not harming others unjustly and enabling them to leave) for political legitimacy. As we saw in chapter 1, libertarians believe that we own ourselves. There we explored the implications of the self-ownership thesis for our ownership rights over things. In chapter 3, when exploring libertarian accounts of minority rights, we noted that, if libertarians are correct, individuals should not be coerced to abide by principles in which they do not acquiesce. This entails that they have the right to choose whether or not to associate with other like-minded individuals. Their right is not a group right, let alone a corporate right. It is, rather, an individual right, which each and every one of us has, to choose the conditions under which we want to associate with others.

The libertarian justification for self-determination, national or otherwise, applies without modification to cases where the individuals who wish to govern themselves make a claim against another community which fails to respect their rights. It also applies to secession cases where they make a claim against another group with which they do enjoy an equal political and juridical relationship. However, philosophers who deploy this particular line of argument are at pains to stress that a demand for self-determination is legitimate if, and only if, (a) no unjust harm would accrue from it to other individuals and groups, and (b) individuals are allowed to exit the community thus established should they wish to do so at a later stage.

We will return to condition (a) below when discussing the territorial dimension of self-determination. As for condition (b), I discussed it in chapter 3, and will not revisit it here. Instead, let me highlight two worries which sceptics might wish to deploy against the libertarian argument for self-determination. First, the argument seems to undercut the very idea of state authority. For it claims that we are bound to obey the state if and only if we consent to it. It seems to follow, then, that, whenever I disagree with the state, I can disobey it. That, however, is a state of anarchy. Indeed, a central objection to Nozick is that the thesis of self-ownership, far from justifying a minimal state, in fact justifies no state at all.

Second, as a number of commentators have averred, the consent argument does not tell us *whose* consent should be sought when deciding whether or not to grant a group of individuals the right to determine their collective future (Brilmayer, 1991; Moore, 2001). Its proponents sometimes claim that it should be sought solely among those individuals themselves (Beran, 1984). And yet, in so far as a decision to secede, or generally to set up one's state, affects third parties, the latter may want to insist that they too should be consulted on the dissolution of the partnership, particularly in those cases where they have not violated the rights of the seceding individuals. At this juncture, a libertarian might be tempted to point out that separation from a group ought to be a unilateral right and that the party which is adversely affected by the separatist's decision to leave can and ought always to be given financial compensation. On that view, the principles regulating self-government are akin to those regulating marriage and divorce: whereas the consent of all parties is required to form an association, the consent of either is sufficient for dissolving it. Unfortunately this will not work. For a claim to national self-determination is not merely a claim to govern oneself along national boundaries, but also a claim to exercise jurisdiction over a particular territory. And just as the principle that the consent of either spouse is sufficient to dissolve a marriage does not *in itself* tell us who should keep the family home, the principle that the consent of a group to set up its own state is sufficient (with other conditions) to grant it statehood does not tell us who, of that group or some other groups, should keep, or get, the disputed territory.

4.2 Territorial claims

This is a good point, then, at which to introduce some standard libertarian justifications for territorial rights. Unsurprisingly, given their friendliness to Locke's defence of private property, libertarian philosophers who seek to provide a justification for territorial rights couch the latter in the language of ownership rights, rather than sovereignty. They acknowledge, of course, that ownership and sovereignty are two different concepts. However, libertarians would maintain, the distinction between sovereignty and ownership should not be overdrawn. After all, one's ownership of a territory is not secured unless one exercises sovereignty over it. Moreover, sovereignty rights look very much like ownership rights: in both cases, decisions have to be made as to whom to allow into country and home respectively, as to how to allocate the wealth one derives from national territory and private land, and so on. With that conceptual point out of the way, then, libertarian justifications for territorial rights appeal to two of the three principles which, as we saw in chapter 1, are constitutive of a theory of distributive justice, namely the principle of transfer and the principle of acquisition.

Hillel Steiner's account of territorial rights is an interesting example of the first kind of justification (Steiner, 1995, 1996). According to Steiner, a community's rights over a piece of territory are reducible to the property rights of the members of that community over it. Suppose that A, B, and C each rightfully own a piece of land. If A and B decide to form an association, and put their pieces of land in common, they acquire joint rights over the territory, T, constituted by both pieces of land. C has decided not to join, and thus does not have a claim over this new territory. So far, so simple. Problems arise, however, several generations later. C's descendants now claim that they ought to have a piece of that territory: since it is not their fault, after all, that their ancestor decided to forego the benefits of that association, they should not be excluded from owning a share of T. Unsurprisingly, A's and B's descendants, who have carried on with the initial association, disagree.

Steiner argues that C's descendants do not have a right to any part of that territory, provided that A and B were the legitimate owners of their respective properties, and that they transferred T to their descendants legitimately. All they have a right to is an *equal* share of the value of the land, which A's and B's descendants are under a duty of justice to give to them. To put the point differently, on Steiner's view, A and B are not under a duty to ensure that C's descendants will get as many opportunities to exercise ownership rights over T: they are not, that is, under a duty to respect the strong variant of the Lockean proviso. Rather, they – and their descendants – are under a duty to ensure that C's descendants have access to a share of the wealth generated on T: they are, that is, under a duty to respect the weak variant of the Lockean proviso.

Now, as we saw in chapter 2 when discussing libertarians' arguments about justice towards generations, whether or not A and B have the right to bequeath T to their descendants very much depends on the theory of rights – choice- or interest-based – which one endorses. Moreover, as we shall see in chapter 7, it is not clear that the claims which individuals now make collectively to exercise sovereignty over a given territory can be properly regarded as claims of inheritance. Setting those two difficulties aside, one still needs an account of the conditions under which A and B acquired their property in the first instance. In other words, appealing to the principle of transfer alone will not do: a justification for territorial rights must also articulate and defend a principle for the rightful acquisition of territory.

Standard libertarian defences of such a principle take two forms, both of which are particularly prevalent in contemporary political discourse. The first – or 'first occupancy argument' – holds that a particular group has a moral right to exercise sovereignty over a given territory because they were the first to occupy it (Gans, 2003; Meisels, 2005). This is one of the claims which Palestinians and Israelis most often make when attempting to show why they should exercise sovereignty over the West Bank and East Jerusalem. At this juncture, though, we must distinguish between two cases. In the first case, (a), the group which is claiming rights over T is a descendant of the first occupant, and occupancy has been continuous over time, so that this group currently occupies T. In the second case, (b), the group which is claiming rights over T is a descendant of the first occupant but does not currently reside – for the most part – on T. To return to our example, some Palestinians argue, as per (a), that their ancestors were the first to occupy Palestine, many thousands of years ago (or, at least, that they occupied it a long time before Jews did), *and* that their occupancy has been continuous since then. In so arguing, they contrast their case for sovereignty over those territories with that of Israelis. For not merely did Jews not occupy Palestine before the Palestinians (or so the latter claim); in addition, Jews *left* Palestine for millennia, which, again according to some Palestinians, considerably weakens their position.

Let us first look at case (a). It will be dismissed by some on the grounds that it is very difficult to identify a clear interest in possessing a territory which would attach specifically to the members of a nation which has first occupied the territory and has done so continuously since. After all, members of other nations who are *also* occupying the territory at present may have a claim too. Suppose that a nation currently resides in a place which they occupied first, and that another nation has invested a part of that territory with huge symbolic significance, even though they were not the first to occupy it. Whether Jews or Palestinians were the first to occupy Israel/Palestine, this particular situation models their present conflict. The first occupancy argument, in this particular case, must explain why what happened further back in the past counts for more than what happened in a more recent past, indeed, than what is happening at present.

In the second case, (b), not only must the group which makes a claim on the basis of first occupancy deal with this difficulty; it must also be able to explain why, given that its ancestors left, it should be allowed to return and to take the land away from those who are currently occupying it. A standard justification for the 'right of return' is that those who left were forced to do so by the land's current occupiers, and that neither they nor their descendants are responsible for the fact that they no longer live there. That fact, it is sometimes thought, provides a strong basis for restituting the territory to those who were expelled, and their descendants. We will examine such claims in chapter 7.

A second libertarian defence of territorial rights appeals not to chronological occupancy, but to what we may call valuable occupancy. In chapter 1, we considered an argument deployed by Locke for private property which relied on the idea that, in labouring over things, one mixes with them something – one's labour – which belongs to them. But in the *Second Treatise of Government*, Locke offers another justification for property rights, which has relevance for territorial claims (1988, §§40–3). There Locke argues that land and natural resources are pretty much worthless unless they are worked on, and that if our labour actually gives value to, say, a piece of land, then it is fair that we should own it. This particular argument is frequently invoked in territorial conflicts. Thus, some Israelis argue that, since they, unlike Palestinians, have managed, by dint of extraordinarily hard work, to create wealth out of a relatively inhospitable land, that land is theirs.

However, supporters of this Lockean justification for territorial rights would need to tackle the following problems. First, what counts as 'adding value' to a piece of land is a controversial issue. Suppose that a country has land which, if turned into a vineyard, would yield very rich harvests; suppose further that the inhabitants of that country have prohibited the production and sale of wine for religious reasons. To them, that land is not a source of wealth, whereas to someone else, it would be (Miller, 1999b). Accordingly, to those who think that adding value consists in wealth creation, that community does not use its land in a valuable way. But to those who think that adding value consists in realizing one's deeply held beliefs, that community is using the land in a valuable way. Under those conditions, it is hard to see how the notion of added value can be used to settle territorial disputes.

Second, Locke's argument presupposes that the territory which is claimed by a national group did not belong to anyone prior to the latter's working on, and adding value to, it. In fact, it is precisely because the territory is not yet owned that acquiring it in that particular way is permitted. If so, however, this argument has very limited applicability, since, more often than not, national communities settle on territories and land which is already occupied by other groups who themselves have already worked on the land, and added value to it – whichever criterion for value one endorses.

To conclude, libertarians do not have – indeed, cannot have – a distinctive theory of *national* self-determination. What they do offer, though, is a distinctive justification for collective self-government, which may or may not be national in character, and which rests on the idea of individual consent to political authority. What they also offer is a distinctive set of arguments in favour of territorial claims.

5 Conclusion

Of our three schools of thought, liberalism is the only one to have a distinctive position on national self-determination. By contrast some strands of communitarianism and libertarianism offer, respectively, reasons to be wary of the view that national belonging is crucial to individual well-being and reasons to endorse the view that individual freedom generates principles of collective, rather than national, self-government.

5 Global Distributive Justice

1 Introduction

In chapter 4, we outlined the conditions under which (according to egalitarian liberals, communitarians, and libertarians) national communities have a claim to constitute themselves into sovereign states with jurisdiction over a given territory. As we will see in chapter 6, deciding whether or not to allow someone legally to settle on their territory is one of the prerogatives which politically self-determining communities are standardly thought to have. Deciding whether or not to transfer some of the wealth which they create to foreigners is another, and will be the focus of this chapter. Some thinkers such as Charles Beitz and Thomas Pogge have advocated extensive, *egalitarian* global distributive policies. Others, such as John Rawls and David Miller, have argued that national communities have duties only to help other countries meet the basic needs of their members and be viable economically.

Needless to say, this issue is far from being merely academic. In fact, it is set against a factual background the reality of which is apparent to all of us. On the one hand, we seem to live in an increasingly globalized world, characterized by a strong economic, political, social, and cultural interconnectedness, and where national political boundaries seem much less relevant than they were, say, thirty years ago. On the other hand, local and national allegiances, projects, and attachments seem to have enduring appeal, as evidenced by nationalistic responses to events such as 9/11 or the fragmentation of the former USSR into nation-states.

This tension between the pull of the global and the attraction of the national, which is the focus of what has become known as the globalization debate (Held and McGrew, 2003), has gone hand in hand (or so some would argue) with a worsening of the economic situation of the world's poor. Whether or not the world's poor are worse off than their counterparts were fifty years ago is one thing; that they do, in absolute terms, live under conditions of severe deprivation is beyond dispute. As Thomas Pogge notes in his influential book *World Poverty and Human Rights*, every year, about 18 million people worldwide die prematurely from poverty-related causes, with a disproportionate number of such deaths arising in Third World countries. Some 46 per cent of humankind live below the World Bank's poverty line, defined as $2 per day. Not only are those people very needy; there are also huge inequalities between the affluent and the poor. Thus, the average income of citizens of affluent countries is fifty times greater in purchasing power than that of the poor; the poorest, those who live below the World Bank poverty line, have about 1.2 per cent of aggregate global income (Pogge, 2002). In effect, we allow distant strangers to live under conditions of deprivation which we would not tolerate at home.

The question, then, is whether we are entitled to do so. Put bluntly, is the tie that binds us to, say, fellow Britons, Germans, Americans, etc., such as to justify the view that we can do more for them than we ought to do for people who are starving in Ethiopia?

The range of positions on offer is as follows:

1 Our obligations of justice towards fellow nationals are the same as our obligations of justice towards foreigners.
2 We have obligations of justice towards both foreigners and fellow nationals, but we owe more to the latter than we do to the former.
3 We have obligations towards fellow nationals and foreigners but, whereas our obligations to the former are obligations *of justice*, our obligations to the latter are more properly called humanitarian obligations.

The first and second positions agree that justice is global in scope, but disagree on the content of our obligations to fellow nationals and foreigners. By contrast, the third position denies that justice is global in scope, and typically asserts, in addition, that we owe more to fellow nationals than we owe to foreigners. In this chapter, we will address the following questions: if you are a luck egalitarian at home, does that mean that you are committed to being a luck egalitarian abroad, or can you argue that, when it comes to helping foreigners, we are under a duty only to meet their needs? If you are an advocate of sufficiency at home, does that mean that you are committed to meeting the needs of foreigners, or can you say that all we owe foreigners is a duty to ensure that they not starve to death, indeed that we owe them absolutely nothing? If you are a communitarian, are you committed to giving priority to the needs and demands of your fellow community members, over those of foreigners? And if you are a libertarian, do you have anything at all to say about obligations to foreigners, except that we simply do not have any?

2 Egalitarian liberalism and global distributive justice

As has been made obvious throughout this book, it is a central tenet of egalitarian liberalism that individuals are worthy of equal concern and respect, irrespective of their race, gender, sexual orientation, and social membership; that they have rights to the protection of their fundamental interests; and that they, and not whatever group(s) to which they belong, are the focus of our concern and respect. Interestingly, however, egalitarian liberals are divided on the all-important question of the scope of justice in the international context. As we shall see in section 2.1, some of them take the principle of fundamental equality to imply that our obligations of justice towards fellow nationals are the same as our obligations of justice towards foreigners. As we shall see in section 2.2, others argue that, whereas justice is global in scope, its content depends on state membership, so that, as a matter of justice, we owe less to foreigners than we owe to fellow nationals or citizens. Finally, as we shall see in section 2.3, others still claim that to conceive of justice as global, rather than domestic, in scope does not make sense. We may call the first and second sets of views 'cosmopolitan', in that they hold that all human beings, wherever they are, have rights against, and obligations to, all other human beings, wherever they are in the world, either directly, or indirectly via international institutional schemes (Pogge, 1992). By contrast, the third view is appropriately thought of as statist, since it holds that the scope of justice extends no further than the boundaries of sovereign states, and that states are the primary site for individuals' rights and obligations.

2.1 Luck egalitarianism, sufficientism, and the irrelevance of borders
The view that we have identical obligations to our fellow nationals and foreigners has been forcefully articulated by a number of philosophers in the last thirty years (see, e.g., Beitz, 1988, 1999; Caney, 2005; Singer, 1972). In this section, I will first describe the implications of Rawls's egalitarian theory of justice as articulated in *A Theory of Justice* for the

distribution of resources between foreigners. I will then expound what I take to be the most plausible radical luck egalitarian and sufficientist arguments in favour of the claim that borders are ethically irrelevant to the determination of who gets what amount of resources.

Let us begin, then, with Rawlsian global justice – by which I mean, to repeat, 'Rawlsian' in the sense of *A Theory*, rather than his later work, which we will examine in section 2.2. As we saw in chapter 1, the point of the original position, and more specifically of the veil of ignorance, is to ensure that individuals choose principles of justice for the allocation of burdens and benefits which will be free of the influence of arbitrary factors such as, for example, natural talents and race. The difference principle is thus meant to nullify the impact of undeserved disadvantages and advantages on individuals' lives.

Now, in his seminal book *Political Theory and International Relations*, Charles Beitz argues that there is no reason not to extend the original position to the world as a whole (Beitz, 1999). If the parties in the original position do not know morally arbitrary facts such as their talents and race, then they ought not to know other morally arbitrary facts about themselves, such as whether or not they live in a country which is richly or poorly endowed in natural resources. Building on Beitz, Pogge makes a similar point and notes that people should be kept in ignorance of their nationality when deciding on principles of justice (Pogge, 1994). For if individuals are ignorant of those facts, they will vote for a distributive framework aimed at minimizing the risks that they might end up badly off simply as a result of living in a poor country. According to those authors, if Rawls's theory of justice is correct at a domestic level, it applies globally, so that the parties should adopt a global difference principle.

Interestingly, for reasons which we will explore in section 2.2 below, Rawls himself disagrees with this view, and develops a non-egalitarian account of what we owe to foreigners. Meanwhile, it pays to note that the Rawlsian view defended by Beitz and others rests on the factual assumption that the world is a scheme of social cooperation. For according to John Rawls, justice is a property of schemes of social and economic interaction, the burdens of which it aims to distribute. In *A Theory of Justice*, the parties in the original position all belong to a single territorially and politically bounded community, the basic institutions of which are the locus for their cooperation. If the theory of justice defended in Rawls's early work is to apply to the world as a whole, then the world as a whole has to resemble such a community. As I noted in section 1, whether it does or not is the subject of fierce debates between proponents of the globalization thesis and sceptics who point to the enduring power of the nation-state. If the sceptics are correct – if, that is, the relationship that obtains between an affluent US citizen and a destitute Somalian is nothing like that which obtains between affluent and destitute US citizens – then there is no reason, within the framework of *A Theory of Justice*, to agree to a global, rather than a domestic, difference principle.

Even if the sceptic is right, there might still be good reasons for endorsing global, non-Rawlsian, egalitarian norms. In chapter 1, we saw that, according to egalitarians, people should not be made worse off, in respect of what makes a life go well, through no fault of their own. Thus, a person's blindness, her lack of remunerative talent, the fact that she is black, or a woman, are morally arbitrary in the sense that she has not chosen them and that they therefore do not in themselves constitute legitimate moral grounds for denying her access to advantages. Inequalities for which individuals are not responsible are to be redressed at the bar of justice, whereas inequalities for which they are responsible are to be allowed. Accordingly, a case for *global* egalitarianism will need to identify a factor which generates inequalities between individuals worldwide. It will also need to explain why individuals are not responsible for the inequalities so generated. Let us address each point in turn.

According to Beitz and Pogge, location in relation to natural resources and nationality (respectively) are the relevant arbitrary, inequality-generating factors. At first sight, that seems right: whether one belongs to resource-rich Saudi Arabia or resource-poor Madagascar crucially affects one's life prospects. Likewise, whether one is a national of wealthy Britain or a national of cripplingly poor Malawi does make a difference. However, generally, whether or not individuals enjoy a high standard of living largely depends on the kind of country in which they *live* – not the kind of country of which they are a national. Moreover, it also depends on whether their country of residence is good or bad at producing wealth – and not on its proximity to natural resources. Accordingly, residence, and neither proximity to natural resources nor nationality, is the most important consideration which should lead us to conceive of distributive justice globally, and not domestically (Fabre, 2007). Furthermore, residence, that is, the fact of living in a given community, is analogous to gender, race, talents, and natural disabilities. If so, then people's access to wealth should not be diminished because they happen to live in a certain kind of community any more than it should be diminished simply because they happen to be of a certain race, or of a certain gender, or because they genetically lack remunerative talents. Thus, on luck egalitarian grounds, well-off individuals, wherever they reside, seem to be under a duty to compensate worse-off individuals, wherever they reside.

I say 'seem to be', because in one crucial respect residence differs from race, gender, and genetic endowments. Whereas we are not in any way responsible for the latter three, we may well have some responsibility for the former. Even if someone is not responsible for being a resident in a country (for example, she is not allowed to emigrate), she may be responsible for the fact that it disadvantages her (for example, she knowingly voted for policies which have depleted the country's resources). Moreover, she may be responsible for the fact that she resides in the country (for example, she can emigrate) and yet she may not be responsible for the fact that staying there disadvantages her (for example, she knowingly voted against unjust policies and yet found herself in the minority). In neither case does she have a claim of justice to resources against residents of other countries. An egalitarian theory of global justice must account for the extent to which individuals can be held responsible for having less access to wealth than residents of other countries.

Needless to say, this is an impossibly difficult task. Whether someone is so responsible depends on whether he has to stay in his country of origin, whether he can leave, whether he has voted for policies which disadvantage him, and so on. Thus, even if justice requires that all inequalities for which people are not responsible be eradicated, irrespective of where they reside in the world, it would not be possible to implement it in practice. The philosophical point to bear in mind, however, is that, under global egalitarianism so conceived, national borders are morally irrelevant: the fact that someone lives within the borders of a given politically self-determining community makes no difference to the strength of their claim to resources against other such communities. On that view, states collect and distribute shares of resources as mandated by justice, and exercise discretion in areas which have little to do with resource distribution (such as sexual morality, medical technologies, etc.), but that is the extent of their right collectively to determine their own future. Moreover, there seems to be nothing, on that particular account, which morally dictates in favour of nation-states as the primary locus for sovereignty. In fact, if it turned out that a world-state would do better at implementing principles of (global) egalitarian justice than the current, Westphalian system, radical luck egalitarians would seem committed to endorsing it.

According to radical egalitarianism, then, foreigners do not have a weaker claim on our resources than our fellow nationals do. This view is shared by a number of philosophers who seem to endorse the sufficiency view (C. Jones, 1999; Nussbaum, 2000; Unger, 1996). Indeed, from the point of view of sufficiency, borders are morally irrelevant too. For if justice requires that individuals have *enough* resources, then again, at first sight, there seems to be no reason at all to restrict the scope of such obligations to those who live within our borders. And that is so however 'enough' is defined. Take the needs-based account of sufficiency. In relation to us, who live in the UK, someone is no less hungry for the fact that she lives in, say, Ethiopia rather than in Glasgow. Likewise, take Anderson's account of the sufficiency threshold, whereby to have enough is to have the resources we need in order to be a fully functioning member of our society. On that view, the fact that someone lacks the resources she needs to be a fully functioning member of Ethiopian society is no less morally pressing for us than the fact that someone lacks the resources she needs in order to be a fully functioning member of British society: the interest in being a fully functioning member of one's society is one which all human beings have, irrespective of which society they live in. Finally, if to have enough means to have the resources we need to fulfil all our human capabilities, as Nussbaum and Sen argue, then, in so far as those capabilities are those of all human beings, it seems that we are under a similar obligation to fellow nationals and foreigners to help them deploy their capabilities (Nussbaum, 2000; Sen, 1992).

The foregoing point needs qualifying in an important respect. Sufficiency thresholds will be set at different heights depending on the level of economic and social development of the countries in question, their geographical location, specific circumstances, etc. This is obviously so for sufficiency defined along Anderson's lines, since what one needs to be a fully functioning member of Ethiopian society is likely to differ from what one needs to be a fully functioning member of British society (Anderson, 1999). Accordingly, taxpayers in the UK will end up transferring more resources to UK residents than they will to residents in Ethiopia. Note, though, that the same goes for sufficiency defined as fairly basic needs: no less obviously, individuals' basic needs for shelter, heating, etc., are not the same in Siberia and Kenya. In that sense, borders are *practically* relevant. But they are not morally relevant. The reason for differential transfers is not that there is a special ethical relationship between, say, UK taxpayers and the needy in the UK. Rather, it is that, in virtue of living in the UK, some individuals have needs which individuals who live in Ethiopia do not, and vice versa. To put the point differently, according to sufficiency theories, borders are relevant to determining what exactly the rich owe to the poor, irrespective of residence. But they are not relevant to establishing that something is owed in the first instance.

Although radical egalitarians and sufficientists can agree that what we *owe*, as a matter of justice, to fellow nationals, we also owe to foreigners, they disagree on one, important point. According to the radical egalitarian view I outlined above, national borders are entirely irrelevant to what we are owed as a matter of justice. This particular view, which we may term radical cosmopolitanism, is compatible with the claim that there are values other than justice which compete with it, such as, for example, the value of national self-determination. As we saw in chapter 1, radical egalitarians are not committed to giving justice priority over all other conflicting values. And they may well, in the end, decide that justice ought to be somewhat compromised for the sake of national self-determination, so that some individuals would end up worse off than others as a result of their residing in a particular country rather than another.

Sufficientist theories of justice, by contrast, are weakly cosmopolitan. They are *cosmopolitan*, in that they too hold that, if we are under an obligation of justice to give enough resources to our fellow nationals, then we are also under an obligation of justice to give enough resources to foreigners. They are *weakly* cosmopolitan, however, because they defend the view that, once the needs of all are met, the well off are not under any obligations to those who are worse off. By implication, they allow national communities to devote all of their remaining resources (once the demands of justice have been satisfied) to collective ventures, projects, and goals of their own. In particular, they allow national communities to do more for their own members than meet their needs. In choosing to distribute their surplus resources in that way, national communities would go beyond what is required by justice at home. The point, though, is that they are permitted to make that choice rather than the different choice of distributing their surplus resources to foreigners. In that sense, at the bar of sufficiency, national belonging can shape the size and content of individuals' bundles of resources, above and beyond what is owed to them as a matter of justice. At the bar of radical equality, by contrast, national belonging may perhaps shape the size and content of individuals' resource bundles, but it does so in violation of justice.

2.2 Egalitarian liberalism and the moral relevance of borders, I: Rawls's Law of Peoples

Contrary to the views which we have just examined, most people believe that borders *are* morally significant to establishing whether we owe anything to others, and that they are significant because national self-determination matters. In section 3, we will assess communitarian arguments to that effect or, at least, arguments which are communitarian in spirit, if not explicitly so. In this sub-section and the next, we will look at two liberal accounts of the significance of borders for the scope of justice. As I noted in section 1 above, philosophers who disagree that our obligations to foreigners are similar to our obligations to fellow nationals take either of the following two views:

1 We have obligations of justice towards both foreigners and fellow nationals, but we owe more to the latter than we do to the former.
2 We have obligations towards fellow nationals and foreigners but, whereas our obligations to the former are obligations *of justice*, our obligations to the latter are more properly called humanitarian obligations.

Quite often, advocates of the first position take a strong egalitarian stand on domestic justice and a non-egalitarian stand towards global justice, so that, while we owe it to fellow nationals to bring about equality, we owe it to foreigners, as a matter of justice, only to ensure that their most basic needs are met. John Rawls's later work, which we examine in this section, can be read along those lines. By contrast, advocates of the second position claim, more strongly, that justice simply *cannot* be global in scope, and that our (humanitarian) obligations to foreigners are less stringent than our (justice) obligations to fellow nationals. We will discuss Thomas Nagel's argument to that effect in section 2.3.

As we saw in section 2.1 above, upon careful reading of *A Theory of Justice*, there seems to be every reason to extend the scope of justice to the world as a whole. However, in his *The Law of Peoples*, Rawls argues against a global difference principle. On his view, the principles of justice which apply domestically are different from those which apply globally: national self-determination matters, according to him, precisely in that it is connected to the notion of responsibility. Imagine a country which saves its resources, with the effect that, two or three generations later, its inhabitants have more than the inhabitants of another country which, at the same time, are conducting consumerist policies. Or imagine a country which fails to check its population

growth, with the effect that, two or three generations later, its inhabitants have less than the members of a country which controlled population growth. Why should the better off, then, subsidize the
irresponsible policies of the consumerist and high population country
(Rawls, 1999b)?

Notice that Rawls's point is a variant on the expensive taste objection, which we encountered in chapter 1. In so arguing, however,
Rawls overlooks the fact that, as the effects of such mistakes may
sometimes only be felt a generation or two later, they are felt by individuals who were not adult, or even born, when those mistakes were
made. By virtue of the principle that people should not be adversely
affected by factors for which they are not responsible, those individuals, presumably, do have a claim for compensation against richer
states. Consider, analogously, the case of two families, in the same
country, of equal size and wealth at time t. Family A saves and is indus-
trious, while family B adopts a leisurely lifestyle, with the effect that
forty years later family A is richer than family B. Rawls nowhere says
in A Theory of Justice, which addresses relationships of justice between
fellow nationals who are members of different families, that families
whose wealth derives from decades of wise investments should not be
taxed in order to compensate poor families whose poverty comes from
decades of money squandering. And indeed, he could not say it, as a
fundamental principle of his is that individuals' claims of justice do
not stem from the family in which they are born, but from their status
as moral equals. By the same token, it seems that Rawls should accept
that an individual member of a consumerist country, whose poverty is
due to management mistakes made before he was born or of adult age,
has a claim against citizens of a frugal country (many of whom, incidentally, benefit from, without having contributed to, wise policies
conducted by their forebears).

Moreover, in the case of a country which does not control its population growth, Rawls's argument implies that the children of those who
failed to check population growth can be denied compensation for
being worse off, on the grounds that their parents could have decided
not to have them. In so far as it disadvantages them for something they
have not chosen themselves, namely for being born in the first place,
it seems that Rawls's principle is unjust, within the Rawlsian framework itself. Outside that framework, however, it chimes in with what I
take to be the most prevalent view on global justice within and without
academia. On that view, we certainly owe it to foreigners to help them
meet their basic needs – indeed we are guilty of an injustice if we fail

to do so, but we are not under any obligation to treat them on a par with our fellow citizens. It is in that sense that, according to Rawls and many others, borders are ethically relevant.

2.3 Egalitarian liberalism and the moral relevance of borders, II: Nagel's political conception of justice

So much, then, for this particular instantiation of the view that our obligations of justice to fellow nationals are distinct from our obligations of justice to foreigners. In this sub-section, we will examine the position, articulated by Thomas Nagel, that the scope of justice is domestic, rather than global. According to Nagel, 'justice is something we owe through our shared institutions only to those with whom we stand in a strong political relation' (Nagel, 2005, p. 121). Moreover, 'beyond the basic humanitarian duties, further requirements of equal treatment depend on a strong condition of associative responsibility . . . such responsibility is created by specific and contingent relations such as fellow citizenship' (ibid., p. 125). Thus, Nagel unambiguously defends what he calls a political conception of justice – the scope of which, to reiterate, extends no further than the borders of sovereign states. Against those who point to the fact that global institutions constitute the basis for shared membership in a particular world order, he writes,

> the absence of sovereign authority over participant states and their members not only makes it practically infeasible for such institutions to pursue justice but also makes them, under the political conception, an appropriate site for claims of justice . . . mere economic interaction does not trigger the heightened standards of socioeconomic justice. (Ibid., pp. 138–9)

And this, in turn, is because justice is a property of organizations which have the authority and legitimacy to impose decisions by force on those who are subject to them. According to Nagel, states are organizations of that kind, whereas global institutions are not, if only because they do not act in the name of individuals but in the name of states themselves.

Although Nagel does not wish to rule out the possibility that global institutions may develop in such a way as to possess the required authority and legitimacy, he believes that this is unlikely to happen and that, if it does, it will cause a great deal of injustice in the process. For Nagel, then, justice is a property of sovereign states, so that, while very needy foreigners have claims to assistance against the well off, their claims are not claims of justice. As can be expected, Nagel's controversial thesis has elicited some criticisms. In particular, it has been criticized for failing to account for the fact that states are already engaged in coercive practices against foreigners (such as, aptly for our purposes in this book, immigration policies), which do have to be justified to them. Accordingly, it is odd to suppose, as Nagel seems to do, that the principles governing those practices cannot be deemed to be principles of justice (Julius, 2006).

Whatever the merits or demerits of Nagel's position, and of the objections which it has attracted, it offers an interesting insight, namely that the principles which regulate our obligations to fellow nationals differ in nature from the principles which regulate our obligations to foreigners.

3 Communitarianism and global distributive justice

Some egalitarian liberals, we noted above, take the view that, in some cases at least, cosmopolitanism must give way to the demands of our fellow community members. In this section, we will assess a communitarian argument to that effect – one which holds that, as a matter of justice, we owe it to foreigners no more than to ensure that their basic needs are met, and that our obligations to them are not obligations of justice. In reaching this conclusion, this communitarian position is similar to some of the views we have already examined. However, it rests on a particularistic understanding of justice, whereby the justifications given for principles of justice, together with the content of those principles, are grounded not in universal values whose normative force transcends borders, but in the distinct cultural and political values of the communities to which they apply.

The view I have in mind has been forcefully articulated by David Miller. As we saw in chapter 4, Miller believes that a state will better perform the task of articulating and implementing principles of justice if it governs a relatively homogeneous and unified nation whose members agree that they are bound together by ties of solidarity. This, in itself, speaks of his scepticism towards demanding principles of global justice – a scepticism which he defends more fully in some of his recent writings (Miller, 1999a, 1999b, 2000, forthcoming). Note that, while Miller himself may resist the label 'communitarian', his position on global justice is sufficiently Walzerian in tone to warrant it in this particular respect. To repeat, it is important to remember that Miller does not deny that we have basic obligations to foreigners such as meeting their basic needs, not exploiting them, and ensuring that they can enjoy some degree of national self-determination. His point, rather, is that this is all that is required of us globally: it does not require more extensive distribution such as meeting more than basic needs, let alone bringing about equality at a global level.

His argument to that effect goes like this. People disagree about three things when they try to formulate a conception of justice: they disagree about the *goods* which fall under the purview of justice, about the *principles* which should regulate the distribution of those goods, and about the *social context* – family, firm, political community – within which the distribution is to occur. Conceptions of justice will vary from one community to another depending on their understanding of each of those three elements, and in particular on their understanding of the first element.

Miller applies that claim to the issue of global justice as follows. Egalitarian principles of global justice impose on very different national communities a universal understanding both of what counts as valuable resources to include as part of a country's wealth *and* of what counts as a need. In so doing, they violate the values of those communities. Let us turn to the first issue – that of what counts as a resource under the purview of justice. To understand Miller's point, consider the following examples (Miller, 1999b; Pogge, 1994). Suppose that a country has land which could be turned into productive vineyards; or suppose that a vast reserve of oil is discovered under Mecca. Secular communities argue that those communities are resource-rich; the latter, however, disagree, on the grounds that, respectively, producing wine and destroying Mecca go against the dictates of their religion. On their view, this land and the oil do not fall within the purview of justice. For the secular communities, they do.

According to Miller, if we are to value the principle that individuals are worthy of respect as producers of social meanings (to use Walzer's phrase), and if we are to attach any importance at all to the institutional instantiation of that principle, namely political self-determination, then we must accede to those communities' request that their land and oil not be considered as part of their endowment in natural resources. This, in turn, implies that those communities ought not to be held under an obligation to compensate other communities for being resource-poor.

We will return to this imaginary scenario later. Meanwhile, sceptics will point to what appears to be a fallacy in Miller's argument. From the claim that those religious communities do not consider their land to have value, he concludes, without further ado, that they *therefore* should not be held accountable for withholding resources which people from other countries might need. In so doing, he seems to assume that the communities actually own the land, and that they should be left to do what they want with it. But this begs the question. Whether or not a community owns the natural resources which are on its territory and the wealth it derives from them is precisely what needs to be established: it cannot be used, as it is by Miller, as an argument in weighing the interests of the religious communities against those of other communities.

Setting that issue aside, note that Miller's theory of justice is particularistic not merely in its understanding of what it means to be resource-rich, but also in its account of what we owe to others. Not only does it deny that justice requires bringing about global equality; it also denies that it requires more than meeting others' basic needs. Its justification for the former view is that we make comparative judgements of *fairness* – is it fair that I have x amount of goods whereas they have $x + 10$? – primarily with fellow nationals and not with non-fellow nationals. Its justification for the latter view is that, in order to decide what justice requires, we must deliberate together, in a democratic forum. Through such deliberation, we can decide what counts as warranting compensation. In particular, we can decide whether lacking a specific resource counts as a need or not. As it happens, Miller argues, such deliberation can only take place within national communities. This is because, in so deliberating, we must be willing to give to people who disagree with us reasons which they can accept. This supposes that there is enough common ground between us and them that we can find such reasons. And it is only within national communities, and not across them, that such ground can be found.

It is easy to see why Miller's critique applies not merely to radical egalitarian views on justice across borders, but also to more modest ones such as the needs-based views we discussed earlier. For if what counts as a need is articulated through deliberative procedures within national communities, it seems to imply that, when it comes to helping foreigners, all we can be sure of is what their *basic* needs are.

For cosmopolitans, Miller's arguments are problematic for the following reasons (Caney, 2003; Fabre, 2003). First, people do make judgements of fairness across borders, for example within supranational entities, such as the European Union. Thus, within Europe, redistribution to poor countries from rich countries is underpinned by an increasing awareness that it is possible to make such comparative judgements of fairness between national communities which, while maintaining many of their national characteristics, belong to the same supranational entity. As I put it elsewhere, '[t]he common agricultural policy, the common fisheries policies, indeed, at global level, humanitarian intervention and refugee policies are all instances where comparative judgements are being made across borders on what people get, give, ought to get, and ought to give' (Fabre, 2003, p. 322).

Second, even if it is true that what counts as a need is best worked out through deliberative procedures within a national community, that does not undermine the view that other communities are under a duty to help meet the needs so defined: community A may have decided, through such procedures, that x is a need, and may well make a claim for help against community B, which does not think that x is a need for its members but may well agree that it counts as a need for A's members.

Third – and this critical remark, if valid, applies not merely to Miller's theory of justice, but to Walzerian theories of justice in general – cosmopolitans, subscribing to universal principles of justice as they do, object that it is rather unclear why the views of the members of a given community determine what counts as a principle of justice. To be sure, trivially, they determine what counts as a principle of justice *for them*; but why should we take that at face value? We do not, in fact Miller himself does not, believe that it is never possible to regard certain practices as unjust, even though those who endorse those practices regard them as just. Accordingly, one needs an argument – which Miller does not seem to provide – as to why meeting foreigners' basic needs is a duty of justice, no matter what, whereas that trying to do more than that, let alone trying to equalize individuals' bundles of resources across borders, cannot count as such.

To conclude, egalitarian liberal proponents of the most demanding (on the affluent) principles of global distributive justice are unlikely to be convinced by Miller's particularistic account of justice. However, they ought to heed what is possibly its most important point – namely that the principles to which they are committed cannot be realized without considerable cost to the value not merely of *national* self-determination, but, more widely, of *political* self-determination. As Miller and his followers will argue, unless radical cosmopolitans are prepared to do away with it almost totally, or to advocate extending it to the world as a whole by way of a global democracy, they must provide an account of which distributive principles – falling short of radical egalitarian principles – would do it justice.

4 A libertarian position: Hillel Steiner on global distributive justice

In sections 2 and 3, we examined egalitarian liberal and communitarian views on what we owe, as a matter of justice, to foreigners. As we saw, they all agree that we owe *something* to foreigners – whether or not our obligations to them are properly deemed to be of justice, and whether or not they encompass more than the duty to ensure that their basic needs are met. Interestingly, very few libertarians have written on this issue. One notable exception is Hillel Steiner, on the basis of whose writings it is possible to articulate a coherent libertarian argument, to the effect that (a) justice is global in scope and (b) individuals owe nothing, as a matter of justice, to foreigners, above and beyond respect for ownership rights (Steiner, 1994). Let us turn, first, to the issue of scope. Libertarians, you recall, argue that all individuals have rights of self-ownership over their person and body, as well as rights of ownership over the resources which they have legitimately acquired or produced. A just social arrangement is one which respects and enforces those rights. On that view, then, a violation of an ownership right is no less unjust for the fact that its victim is a foreigner. As Steiner points out, we all have a right to an equal portion of initially unowned things. If so,

> like the incidence of self-ownership rights, the equality mandated by this right is global, not local. Red owes duties correlative to this right to White [his compatriot] as well as to Blue [a foreign national]. It's not sufficient that he allow an equal portion of these things to only Blue and each of their compatriots: he must also respect White's and everyone else's similar entitlement, regardless of where on the globe they are. The fact that where they are is on the far side of some international boundary no more licences them to deprive them of these entitlements than it does to shoot them. (Steiner, 1994, p. 265)

Note, however, that, although borders are irrelevant to determining individuals' *initial* entitlements to unowned things, they can be highly relevant to determining their entitlements at some later stage. As we saw in chapter 4, at the bar of libertarian justice, individuals are entitled to form politically self-determining communities with other like-minded individuals, provided that they respect the Lockean proviso. But the Lockean proviso, you recall, admits of two variants. On the strong variant, one is entitled to appropriate a resource if one leaves others with as many, and similar, opportunities to appropriate resources. On the weak variant, one is entitled to appropriate a resource if one leaves others with as many opportunities to use things.

Those different interpretations of the Lockean proviso will yield different accounts of entitlements across borders. Imagine a community of individuals, C, which appropriates fertile land – say, to return to one of our earlier examples, land which could yield rich grape harvests – with a view to forming a self-determining community. If libertarian justice requires that they respect the strong Lockean proviso, and if they do leave other individuals and communities opportunities to appropriate similarly rich land, then they are entitled to withhold the proceeds of the grape harvests from them. In so far as those other individuals and communities had similar opportunities to create wealth, they lack a claim to resource transfers from C. Whether or not one belongs to C, then, will determine whether or not one has rights over the resources appropriated by C.

Suppose, by contrast, that libertarian justice requires only that C respect the weak variant of the proviso. As we noted in section 4 of chapter 4, C *can* appropriate all of the fertile land that there is, provided that it transfers to outsiders equal shares of the value of that land. On that view, C is under an obligation of justice to transfer resources to foreigners. If it does so, then it is entitled to hold on to the land. This implies, in turn, and here again, that whether or not someone belongs to C does determine the content of his bundle of resources. If he does belong to C, he will enjoy rights to control, use, sell, etc., the territory which C appropriated. If he does not belong to C, he will not enjoy such rights, but instead enjoy rights to an equal share of the monetary value of that territory.

In both cases, community membership, and thus borders, affects which ownership rights individuals have. This, however, is compatible with the libertarian claim that individuals are not owed anything, as a matter of justice, if their ownership rights (over themselves and over legitimately acquired resources) are respected. Nor does it undermine Steiner's claim that justice is global, rather than domestic, in scope. For the fact that community membership determines the content of individuals' resource bundles has nothing whatsoever to do with national or political borders. Put differently, the Lockean proviso applies to any appropriation, be it by one individual, an association of two individuals, or a community of individuals united by common nationality. Conversely, the ownership rights which, according to libertarianism, a just society must protect are those of individuals, irrespective of community or association membership. Thus, suppose that a British citizen discovers on his own some hitherto unowned piece of land, and appropriates it (for example, and consistent with libertarian views on legitimate acquisition, by being the first to occupy it, or by working on it). His obligations under the Lockean proviso, whichever version of the proviso one endorses, are to fellow British citizens *and* to foreign nationals. Were he to appropriate the land and share its value equally between fellow British citizens only, on the grounds that he and they belong to the same national community, he would violate the libertarian thesis that all individuals, irrespective of their race, gender, and, by extension, community membership, have equal rights over unowned material resources.

5 Conclusion

To conclude, we have reviewed a wide range of positions on the global justice debate. Interestingly, some egalitarian liberals and communitarian-minded philosophers agree that all we owe to foreigners as a matter of justice is to help them meet their basic needs, but differ in the way they reach this conclusion. No less interestingly, radical egalitarians and libertarians agree that borders are ethically irrelevant to our duties to one another.

Finally, our study of the global justice debate suggests that there is a tension between two competing principles. On the one hand, cosmopolitanism – in its radical egalitarian or libertarian forms – holds that all human beings, wherever they are, have equal rights to resources or to appropriate them. On the other hand, ethical particularism holds that individuals are entitled to give priority to their fellow community members when allocating rights and freedoms. In the next chapter, we will see those two principles at play in the philosophical literature on immigration.

6 Immigration

1 Introduction

In chapter 3, we examined a number of positions on the claims which immigrants sometimes make against the government of the country in which they have settled. However, we did not outline the conditions under which, according to those positions, immigrants ought to be, or can be, allowed in. Nor did we do so in chapter 4, where we outlined various stands on the view that national communities have a claim to govern themselves as independent sovereign states. It is this particular question, immigration, which is the focus of this chapter.

Curiously, philosophers have neglected immigration, notwithstanding its claim to being one of the most important political issues of our time. The 1990s saw a sharp rise in the number of claims for asylum in Western countries, as well as in the number of refugees worldwide. According to recent figures released by the United Nations High Commission for Refugees, there were, as of late 2005, about 10 million refugees, asylum seekers and stateless persons, as well as a further 10 million individuals who, while not falling in any of those three categories, nevertheless are deemed to be 'of concern' to the UNHCR (UNHCR, 2006). Incidentally, and contrary to popular perception in the West, the highest proportions of refugees live not in Western countries, but in poorer countries with their own severe economic difficulties, such as Pakistan, Congo, and Sudan.

Faced with thousands of would-be immigrants, states – particularly wealthy states – try to restrict entrance, partly in response to their populations' hostility to immigrants, partly for reasons to do with foreign policy and security concerns. The aim of this chapter is to address the following question: according to egalitarian liberals, communitarians, and libertarians, on what moral grounds, if any, can a state legitimately refuse entrance on its territory to potential immigrants? To

answer that question, one must get an understanding of what is at
stake. In particular, one needs to draw a distinction between four different categories of entrants: refugees, asylum seekers, economic
migrants, and relatives of individuals who are already settled in a
foreign country (Gibney, 2004). According to the UNHCR definition,
a refugee is someone who was forced out of his or her country of
nationality by fears of persecution on grounds of religious or political
beliefs, or of membership in a political group, and who cannot return
there on pain of being subject to such persecution. As has often
been noted, this definition arbitrarily excludes from the category of
refugees those individuals who are forced out of their country because
of wars and famines, and who cannot return on pain of losing their
lives. For our purposes here, then, a refugee is anyone who has been
forced out of his or her country of origin by life-threatening events,
and who would die if he or she were to return.

Refugees typically live in transit border camps. In this, they are distinct from asylum seekers, who are also exposed to lethal dangers if
they return to their own country, but are already at the border of a safer
state. Standardly, while host states can, in international law, refuse to
take refugees from transit camps, they cannot physically turn away
refugees who present themselves at their borders, if sending them
back would expose them to life-threatening dangers. The principle of
non refoulement is a central plank of the UN 1951 Convention Relative
to the Status of Refugees (article 33), and implies that geographical
proximity to a host state is relevant to delineating the latter's obligations to entrants. We will have to assess the grounds for this distinction later on. In both cases, we will have to touch on a crucial question.
Refugees and asylum seekers, as we saw, are forced out of their
country by persecution, wars, and famines, and would face the same
life-threatening predicament if they were to return. More often than
not, they have had to leave because their fundamental human rights
have been violated, and would be subject to similar violations if denied
protection by other states. In other words, host countries are called
upon to help where home countries have failed in their duties to their
own members. Whether or not host countries are under a duty, to foreigners, to shoulder the costs of their governments' dereliction is one
of the most difficult points at issue.

A third category of entrants is that of economic migrants, who do
not face death in their country of origin, but who seek to make a better
life elsewhere. They range from the high-flying Indian lawyer who
would rather practise in Toronto than New Delhi, to the Polish

carpenter who cannot find work in Warsaw and who, keen to improve his and his family's quality of life, migrates to London in search of work and higher wages, to the Vietnamese farmer who, while not facing death by starvation in his country, nevertheless can only just secure his own subsistence, and takes the highly risky trip, via the back of a lorry and in the hands of unscrupulous middlemen, to Europe. In so far as the needs of those migrants (if, in the case of the lawyer, they can even be described as needs) are less pressing than those of refugees, we shall have to see whether they have any claim at all to being granted entrance into their chosen country of emigration.

Finally, a large number of those who make an entrance claim against Western countries are relatives of individuals who are already settled in a host country. Those countries have often been more generous towards these groups than towards economic migrants, on the understandable grounds that families belong together, particularly spouses and parents and children. However, here again, we will have to assess whether it is legitimate for a host country to turn away economic migrants such as our Vietnamese farmer, in order to take in the extended family of our Indian lawyer.

Not only do we need to distinguish between different categories of immigrants; we also need to differentiate between two different understandings of immigration. The debate on immigration is sometimes couched, in the relevant academic literature, in terms of freedom of movement. Yet, when we prevent foreigners from settling in our country, we do not merely impede their freedom of movement; we also deny them *membership* in our political community, with its attendant benefits and entitlements. At one extreme, to deny entrance to a stateless person is tantamount to denying her the bare minimum which states normally provide to their residents, namely the legal protection of her rights. At the other extreme, to deny entrance to a high-flying professional is to deny her the benefit of living, and working, in the country of her choice. In both cases, the would-be entrant is denied not so much a freedom, but the good of membership and its basic feature, namely lawful settlement on a territory. Accordingly, there are two ways of framing the question of immigration. We can think of it as the freedom to move across borders, in which case our question becomes that of the kind of restrictions, if any, which we can and, according to some authors, should, impose on it. Or we can think of it as pertaining to the distribution of the good of membership, in which case our question becomes that of the principles to which its distribution can and should be subjected (Coleman and Harding, 1995).

A final point before I begin. There might be other ways than immigration to remedy the plight of outsiders. Thus, some philosophers argue that, rather than taking increasing numbers of refugees and economic migrants, host nations should act in such a way as to ensure that those individuals have no reason to knock on their door in the first instance. Most obviously, they should stop supporting repressive regimes. Others argue, in line with the arguments we examined in chapter 5, that host nations should transfer some of their resources to poorer countries (Barry, 1992). Be that as it may, it is unquestionably true that countries which are in a position to host immigrants do neither. Consequently, it is imperative to turn our attention to the ethical issues raised by immigration. I will start by constructing Rawlsian and egalitarian liberal positions on open borders (section 2), followed by communitarian and libertarian arguments (sections 3 and 4 respectively). As we will see, egalitarian liberalism and libertarianism, unlike the communitarian position we will examine, both make space for the view that, under certain conditions, countries are under a duty to allow immigrants in. The interesting question, then, is that of how to allocate immigrants among host countries. I will say a few words about it in section 5. But I will not address in any detail the question of what kind of membership states ought to confer on would-be immigrants – whether, for example, they should (depending on which of our overarching three frameworks one endorses) give them full political rights, or whether they should restrict their access to welfare benefits otherwise available to host citizens. Rather, my concern is with delineating the conditions under which states can, indeed perhaps ought to, allow would-be immigrants to cross their borders and settle legally on their territory.

2 An egalitarian liberal case for relatively open borders

2.1 A Rawlsian view on immigration

Although Rawls's writings on political liberalism are motivated, at least in part, by the fact that societies are culturally and ethnically plural, and thus by the fact of immigration, he does not offer a justification for, or against, restrictions on immigration. But it is nevertheless possible to glean what a Rawlsian view on immigration would look like, where, by Rawlsian, one means, here again, 'faithful to *A Theory of Justice*'. Let us remind ourselves of the central tenets of Rawls's theory of justice:

1   Society is a scheme of social cooperation where we can each advance our conception of the good life. We live together, impose burdens on each other, and create benefits. We need principles to allocate those burdens and benefits, and those principles are principles of justice.

2   When choosing those principles, we ought not to be guided by arbitrary factors such as our conception of the good, our talents, our gender, or our race. To that end, we put ourselves in a hypothetical situation – the original position – and imagine how we would allocate burdens and benefits if we did not know who we are and where we come from.

3   The principles we choose behind the veil of ignorance are the *liberty principle* (each individual has a right to enjoy basic liberties, consistent with a similar and equal right for others), the *equal opportunity principle* (offices and positions are open to all), and the *difference principle* (social and economic inequalities are permitted provided they benefit the worst-off members of society).

4   The liberty principle is lexically prior to the difference principle. That is, restrictions on liberty are permitted only for the sake of securing liberty itself, not for the sake of bringing about material equality. Finally, the liberty principle includes fundamental, standardly liberal rights, such as liberty of conscience, private property, not being tortured, not being killed arbitrarily, and, crucially for our purpose here, *freedom of movement.*

At first sight, it might seem that Rawls's methodological device – the original position – is not particularly suited to the question of immigration, simply because movements of individuals on such large scales are, more often than not, the result of failure on the part of the latters' governments to secure their basic rights. As Rawls is at pains to stress, his theory of justice is not meant to deal with such cases. Rather, it is meant to regulate what individuals owe to each other within so-called well-ordered societies, where there are enough resources to ensure that people do not face immediate starvation, and where there is enough stability that whichever principles the parties agree on would be enforced and respected.

Although Rawls's methodology does not provide much guidance where refugees and asylum seekers are concerned, it delivers interesting results in the case of economic migrants and family members. When discussing the issue of global distributive justice in the previous chapter, we saw that Rawls assumes, in *A Theory of Justice*, that individuals in the original position are members of the same nation-state. We also saw that a number of philosophers have rejected this as an arbitrary restriction on the scope of justice. On their view, parties in the original position should not know which country they come from. Suppose, for the sake of argument, that this is correct. The question at issue here is what the parties would choose with respect to immigration. As they are risk-averse and do not know anything about their personal circumstances, it seems that they would opt for a policy of relatively open borders. If one does not know which country one resides in, one does not know whether one will need to settle in another country for economic or political reasons. Under those circumstances, it makes sense to extend freedom of movement across borders.

Furthermore, in so far as the right to freedom of movement is part of the liberty principle, it ought to be distributed equally. This suggests that all individuals should have equal rights to move around freely across borders. Besides, it is prior to the difference principle, and therefore can be restricted only for the sake of liberty itself. Consequently, the parties would say, in all likelihood, that they should be allowed to move from one country to the next, without restrictions, unless freedom of movement would be detrimental to the exercise of liberty itself. In making that choice, they would rule out restrictions on immigration which are justified on economic grounds (such as 'we cannot take foreigners in because our extensive distributive policies depend on operating in a relatively homogeneous community'). However, they would allow restrictions on immigration which are justified by appealing to the preservation of liberty itself, so that would-be immigrants who would pose a threat to individual liberty would be denied entrance. In this, our construal of a Rawlsian position on immigration chimes in with a worry (to which we will return in section 2.3 below) which many politicians, policy-makers, and citizens alike express when faced with an influx of immigrants from illiberal cultures.

Suppose, however, that the question of immigration ought to be understood not as a matter of freedom of movement, but as the question of how to distribute the good of membership (which confers access to income and wealth) in a politically self-determining community. If immigration is seen in those terms, there does not seem to be any reason not to subject the distribution of that good to the difference principle. Thus, everyone, wherever they come from, should be allowed to move around freely, unless restrictions on freedom of movement would benefit the worst off. On that view, such restrictions as based on economic reasons (to the effect that better off immigrants would take away jobs from the poorest of our citizens) would be justified, unless it could be shown that immigrants would in fact contribute enough to their host country's gross domestic product, and thus to tax payments, so as to benefit the worst off in those countries. (This is in fact arguably the case, according to recent governmental figures, in most Western European countries.)

In short, whether we conceive of immigration in terms of freedom of movement across borders, or in terms of the distribution of membership, there are good reasons to think that Rawlsian justice dictates in favour of open borders, with two qualifications. Restrictions on immigration are permitted if open borders would (a) jeopardize the preservation of liberty itself and (b) benefit the worst off.

> ʌ Fail to

2.2 Egalitarian liberal arguments for open borders

In section 2.1, we examined a Rawlsian position on immigration. In this section, we assess a liberal case for open borders as made by Robert Goodin and Joseph Carens. Their case does not appeal to choices which parties would make behind the veil of ignorance. Rather, it appeals to a series of three analogies: between goods and individuals, between allowing people to leave our community and allowing them to join in, and between freedom of movement within our borders and freedom of movement across them (Carens, 1992; Goodin, 1992). Before exploring their arguments in greater detail, it is worth pointing out that, on their view, the fourfold distinction between immigrants, asylum seekers, economic migrants, and family members is irrelevant, since *everyone*, irrespective of their own particular set of circumstances, has a *prima facie* right to settle in the country of their choice.

Now, according to the first of those three arguments, if we allow the movement of goods across borders, as we indeed already do, then it is hypocritical not to allow movements of individuals across borders. However, this argument raises the following three issues. First, material goods and individuals are different in many ways, and in such ways as to undermine the argument. Most obviously, letting people in has economic and social consequences which letting goods in does not. More specifically, bringing new people into a given community may well change its fabric in profound ways. Goods and money do not have the same effect. Second, and relatedly, while the completely free exchange of goods is likely to benefit both parties involved in the transaction, the completely free movement of people may not benefit the receiving community. Third, one may query the premise on which the argument rests, namely that we ought to allow the movement of goods across borders. As a matter of fact, most countries do not do so, and in fact safeguard their markets by taking highly protectionist measures against the importation of cheaper goods from other countries. As a matter of principle, many would argue that those measures are justified, on the grounds, for example, that they protect the livelihood of our farmers. And if that argument is correct, then there is a case for restricting the movement of people across borders.

The second strand of the standard liberal case is that, if we allow our fellow members to leave our community, then we ought to allow outsiders to join in. More generally, if we think that the right to exit is fundamentally important, we have to recognize that so is the right to join, since a right to exit without anywhere to go is meaningless. We encountered that argument when discussing Kukathas's libertarian position on special minority rights in chapter 3. In the context of immigration, however, the argument is problematic in the following respect. Although it is true that a right to exit without anywhere to go is meaningless, it is unclear why it imposes an obligation on wealthier countries to take other people in. To use and adapt an example I gave in that chapter, the claim that the Roman Catholic Church ought to allow its members to leave the church does not imply that it ought to take in dissidents from other churches. Likewise, the fact that liberal states are committed to letting their own members out does not imply that they should be committed to letting foreigners in. In fact, they might argue, there are very good reasons for not letting foreigners in, even though we let our own members out, namely that doing the former is far more burdensome, economically and culturally, than doing the latter.

The third strand of the standard liberal case is that, if we allow freedom of movement *within* our borders, and in particular if we allow people to change their place of residence and to settle anywhere within their own country, then we should allow it *across* them. This, of course, is appealing, as it invokes the cherished liberal freedom to go wherever we want within our country. To claim that we do not have the right to do so conjures up pictures of Soviet citizens who were not allowed freely to move from one part of the Soviet Union to another without an internal passport. Here again, though, the liberal case assumes that the costs which a host nation may have to pay if it allows everyone in are similar to the costs which a region or town may have to pay if all of the country's residents are allowed to settle there. According to many critics, this is simply not the case.

To conclude, this liberal argument is problematic because the analogies on which it rests are not quite satisfactory.

2.3 Open borders and distributive justice: sufficiency and immigration
Liberals who are critical of this three-pronged argument for open borders have the resources to mount another case for allowing foreigners in. In chapter 5, we examined the view that wealthy nations are under a duty of justice to give to foreigners enough material resources (depending on one's reading of sufficiency) to function fully as a member of society, or to enjoy the full range of human capabilities. Suppose, though, that such transfers will not yield the required result: corruption at governmental level diverts funds from intended beneficiaries; the needy do not so much need material resources as a safe haven to escape civil and political oppression, etc. Suppose further that, in those cases, allowing the needy in will do the trick. If so, opening borders is owed to them, *prima facie,* as a means to avoid oppression, and as a remedial measure in cases where material distribution will not give them the resources they need (see, e.g., Perry, 1995).

If the foregoing point is correct, it suggests that a host government, when deciding whom to allow in, should give priority to the neediest individuals. Refugees and asylum seekers would have a stronger case than economic migrants or relatives of immigrants whose plight is far less serious. As we saw above, though, such an approach conflicts with the view that *all* individuals have a right to free movement. Some commentators take this to undermine the open border view. For on that view, as we saw, it does not seem right to discriminate on the basis of need. And surely, the criticism goes, refusing to discriminate on the basis of needs is counter-intuitive: how can the Vietnamese farmer who can secure the means only for basic subsistence in his own country *not* be given priority over the high-flying barrister who would rather practise in Toronto than New Delhi (Gibney, 2004)?

This point is made against proponents of open borders who conceive of immigration as a matter of freedom. However, it is vulnerable to the criticism that there is nothing incoherent in holding on the one hand that all individuals have a *prima facie* right to be allowed in on grounds of freedom of movement, and on the other hand that, if they cannot *all* be allowed in, at least *some of them* should be allowed in on the basis of needs.

So, to recapitulate, material neediness might well provide a better reason than the aforementioned analogies for holding wealthier nations under a duty to open their borders. The question, then, is whether there are considerations to be deployed against a right of entry. From within the sufficiency view, some deploy economic and cultural arguments in favour of restricting immigration. Foremost among those is the claim that taking in more immigrants will threaten the host country's ability to provide for the needs of its members, in two ways. First, the number of claimants on the welfare state will rise, as a result of which fewer resources will be available towards meeting needs. Second, cultural diversity is not conducive to fostering the kind of solidarity on which the welfare state depends.

This objection to the right of entry shares with the needs-based case for open borders the view that meeting the needs of the destitute is important. However, it holds that, if taking in immigrants would adversely affect our prospects for alleviating poverty among our co-nationals, then we cannot be held under a moral duty to do so. This is because, just as individuals have the prerogative not to sacrifice their weighty interests for the sake of another person, communities have the prerogative to ensure that their own members do not sacrifice their weighty interests (in a basic standard of living) for the sake of for-eigners. We already encountered that point in the previous chapter. Empirically, however, most economists agree that immigration tends to strengthen, rather than weaken, host economies. Immigrants, they argue, tend to be young, and seek work in areas where there is a short-age of skilled, or willing, workers. Moreover, they help expand domes-tic markets for consumer goods, contribute taxes, help reduce the demographic gap between the young and the old, and so on. And while they make demands on the welfare state (in that they need help with, for example, medical care and housing), available data from rele-vant governmental departments in Western countries show that immigrants contribute more to Western economies than they take from them (Dummett, 2001; Gibney, 2004; Simon, 1989).

Cultural considerations are sometimes brought to bear against opening up borders. A standard argument to that effect holds that a state has a right to turn away immigrants if the latter would rapidly submerge its national culture. Even the staunchest proponents of open borders, such as Michael Dummett, concede the point. Human beings, they accept, are very attached to their own culture. This does not mean that they have a right that it should never change under the influence of new entrants. But it does mean that they have a right that it not disappear quickly (Dummett, 2001). However, Dummett also stresses that a gradual increase in the amount of entrants into those states would not threaten the national culture. Even if his concession is sound, then, it justifies far fewer restrictions on immigration than states, and in particular European states, are keen to enforce.

A similar point can be made on a variant of this cultural argument against open borders, which we encountered when discussing a Rawlsian perspective on immigration, and which goes like this: 'we live in a liberal regime; if we allow illiberal people in, our liberal culture will be threatened; so we should be allowed to exercise discretion.' Here again, this argument, even if sound, justifies looser restrictions on immigration than its proponents think it does, since it would have to show that allowing some people in would threaten the very survival of the liberal culture. Accordingly, turning away a single illiberal immigrant would not be justified; turning away small groups would not be justified either. Turning away very large groups of illiberal immigrants might be. Where to draw the line between acceptable and unacceptable (from a liberal point of view) rates of entry is beyond the scope of this book.

Before turning to communitarian views on immigration, let me say a few words about the issue of the so-called 'brain drain'. When describing economic migrants, I gave the example of a high-flying Indian lawyer who would rather practise law in Toronto than in New Delhi. Closer to reality are those scores of qualified professionals from Third World countries – teachers, nurses, doctors – who, every year, seek and find employment in Western countries. It is in fact fair to say that the British National Health system has become increasingly dependent on this particular labour force, whose skills are needed as much, if not considerably more, in their countries of origin than they are here. (Although those workers send remittance payments to their families, and thus contribute in very important ways to the latter's welfare – a primary reason why they emigrate in the first instance – skill shortages in their countries of origin remain a serious problem.) The question, from a sufficientist (or, indeed, egalitarian) theory of justice, is whether wealthier nations are morally entitled to grant entry to those individuals, for the sake of their own members, at the cost of the severely poor abroad. At first sight, it might seem that they are so entitled, for example on the grounds of freedom of movement, or on the grounds that, up to a point at least, wealthier nations are permitted to give priority to the needs, or opportunities, of their members over those of foreigners. Suppose, however, that wealthy nations are under an obligation of justice to ensure that the needs of individuals from other countries are met. On that view, one may be leaning towards restricting the freedom of movement of those individuals whose contributions in kind to their own people is vital to the latter. Or one might end up defending the view that for wealthy nations to drain poor nations of their professionals is morally acceptable if, and only if, the former compensate the latter for the resulting loss, by way of increased resource transfers.

3 A communitarian position: Walzer on immigration

As we saw in chapter 1, communitarians criticize liberalism for overlooking the importance of community membership in the formation of individual identity, and insist that individuals cannot stand back from their community membership – widely defined – in the way liberals say they can. As we also saw in chapters 4 and 5, some communitarian thinkers, such as Walzer, privilege membership in the larger, political, national community. By contrast, others, such as McIntyre, confer greater weight on communal sources of identity such as the family, the neighbourhood, and the tribe. In the absence of specifically communitarian writings on immigration (with the exception of Walzer's *Spheres of Justice*, which we will examine presently), construing *a* communitarian position on this particular issue is no easy task. Thus, it is rather hard to discern how someone such as McIntyre would view current restrictions as imposed on immigration by wealthier nations. For if the neighbourhood, rather than the nation itself, is an important source of identity for individuals, on what grounds can the British government prevent extended families and friends of, say, Bangladeshi individuals, who are already settled in the UK, from entering the UK? At the same time, however, McIntyre would in all likelihood be reluctant to endorse the view that those individuals have *a right* to be allowed to settle legally in the UK.

In this, Walzer's position, as he articulates it in chapter 2 of his *Spheres of Justice*, has the benefit of clarity. As Walzer writes, 'the distinctiveness of cultures and groups depends upon closure and, without it, cannot be conceived as a stable feature of human life. If this distinctiveness is a value, as most people . . . seem to believe, then closure must be permitted somewhere' (Walzer, 1983, pp. 39f.). States, in that respect, are analogous to clubs: they cannot prevent their members from leaving, but they can prevent them from joining. In another respect, they are like families: just as families look after their own, so do states, and, when it comes to immigration decisions, they are entitled to privilege the foreign relatives of current, natural- ized, citizens.

Let us assess Walzer's argument for states' extensive rights to restrict immigration. Sceptics will seize on the following issues. First, they will argue that the analogy between the state and the family loses its appeal once one sees that the ties of affection which bind family members do not exist between co-nationals. It is in virtue of those ties that family members are entitled to privilege one another (up to a point) over outsiders. Absent those ties between the members of a national group, further argument is needed to show that those members are entitled to privilege one another over foreigners, includ- ing when deciding who will become a member in the first instance.

Second, the analogy between states and clubs is not as powerful as it seems, if one concedes – as many people do – that there are, in fact, moral restrictions on how clubs ought to behave. Golf clubs in the USA and traditional clubs in the UK, for example, have been chal- lenged over race-based and gender-based membership restrictions. Although a critic of Walzer may not want to go as far as to say that clubs should be legally barred from making such decisions, he may perhaps want to go as far as to say that they are acting wrongly. Analogously, then, he may want to say that states are not morally per- mitted to act as they please when it comes to regulating immigration. Moreover, and more importantly still, the analogy between states and clubs founders on the rather obvious point that being denied mem- bership in a club is not quite the same, to put it mildly, as being denied membership in a state, particularly when one is an economic migrant on the downward side of the needs scale, let alone a refugee or an asylum seeker. At its most extreme, to be denied entry into a safe state is to be confronted with the likelihood that one will be per- secuted or starved to death. Walzer is aware of that point, of course, and claims that states ought not to turn away refugees and asylum seekers, on the grounds that they ought to abide by the universal principle of mutual aid. Thus, he criticizes the White Australia policy adopted by the Australian government (whereby non-white immi- grants were not allowed into Australia) on the grounds that the very acute needs of non-whites did, in fact, override the Australians' wish for a homogeneous society. However, it is very unclear how Walzer can reconcile his rejection of the White Australia policy with his broader theory of justice. Remember two very important statements he makes at the end of *Spheres of Justice*: 'a given society is just if its substantive life is lived in a certain way – that is, in a way faithful to the shared understanding of its members' (1983, p. 313). And later: 'Justice is rooted in the distinct understandings of places, honors, jobs, things of all sorts, that constitute a shared way of life. To override those understandings is (always) to act unjustly' (ibid., p. 314). So, by those tokens, if white Australians understand membership in their community as informed by race, it would be unjust to impose on them a different understanding of what community membership *per se* is. Walzer, here again, faces a dilemma which many communitarians whose politics are liberal also face: namely, how to reconcile impeccably liberal prescriptions (such as the universal principle of mutual aid) with a communitarian meta-theory of justice.

Moving away from the specific features of Walzer's position, it is worth pointing out that any communitarian stand on immigration is likely to invoke the view that cultures – be they national or local cultures – are entitled, as such, to their own preservation, and thus are entitled to reserve entry to those who share their religion, ethnicity, moral values, and so on. In this respect, the communitarian position is congenial to popular views (at least in the West) on immigration. The French, for example, are more welcoming of white and Catholic Poles than they are of Muslim Algerians. However, communitarians do not really provide an argument as to why individuals are entitled to the protection of their culture, and, in particular, are entitled to close it off to outsiders who, precisely because they are outsiders, might transform and change it (Perry, 1995).

Moreover, it is worth noting that the communitarian argument in favour of cultural preservation works only if potential host communities have a legitimate claim to control access to the particular territory which they inhabit (Gibney, 2004). As we saw in chapter 4, by denying someone entry into our country, we are in fact denying them the possibility of lawfully occupying a particular piece of territory. If we lack a claim to that territory in the first instance, we lack the right to forbid them to settle there – and this irrespective of whether they are refugees, asylum seekers, economic migrants, or family members of existing immigrants. In so far as the rights of the wealthiest nations over the territory which they occupy are morally dubious to say the least, their claim that they are entitled to turn would-be entrants away from that territory is equally dubious.

To summarize, communitarianism is faced with a number of difficulties when justifying communities' wish to control admission in their midst. Notwithstanding those difficulties, however, it brings home a tension, which we encountered in chapter 5, between the two competing principles of cosmopolitanism and particularism.

4 A libertarian position: Hillel Steiner on immigration

As we have just seen, communitarian accounts of justice in immigration confer extensive rights on political communities to close their borders to would-be newcomers. Unsurprisingly, in the light of our overviews of libertarian theories of multiculturalism and national self-determination, libertarians would assent. Consider Hillel Steiner's take on this issue. Steiner asks us to imagine a community of individuals who own summer cottages by a lake. Each cottage has its own access to the lake, but there is a common beach, as well as common facilities. Individuals have acquired the cottages by buying them from someone who owned the whole estate; when buying them, they acquired collective rights over the common facilities, as well as the right to veto the acquisition of other cottages by outsiders. In effect, then, they are given the right to control who joins their community of holiday-makers. This real-life example, Steiner claims, is analogous to decisions on immigration. If one thinks that this community is entitled to turn away outsiders, then any given state is entitled to turn away prospective immigrants. And if one thinks that the community is entitled to grant admittance to one or several of the cottages, then, similarly, any given state is entitled to grant entry to prospective immigrants (Steiner, 1992).

As should be clear, this libertarian argument assumes that ownership is the same thing as sovereignty. As we saw in chapter 4, however, those notions are distinct, and the mere fact that we jointly own the territory on which we live may not be enough to confer on us the sovereign right to exclude others. In any event, states' claim to restrict entry and exclude foreigners is extremely weak, at the bar of libertarian principles. Remember Nozick's theory of entitlements: 'The holdings of a person are just if he is entitled to them by the principles of justice in acquisition and transfer, or by the principle of rectification of injustice . . . If each person's holdings are just, then the total set (distribution) of holdings is just' (Nozick, 1974, p. 153). So, if my holdings are just, if, that is, I have a legitimate title to my property, then I can refuse entry to anyone. Similarly, if a state has a rightful claim to exercise sovereignty over its territory, for example on the grounds that its members have added value to the land, or have been the first to occupy it and yet have respected the Lockean proviso, it can deny entry to prospective immigrants.

But if that is so, then, and as we saw when discussing Nozick's theory of justice in chapter 1, very few people can claim to have legitimate entitlements to their property. Even if they acquired it from someone else legitimately, it is likely that, at some point, the chain of legitimate transfers got broken, and that the property came into someone's hands illegitimately. In so far as, according to libertarians, a state's territorial rights are simply the concatenation of its individual members' rights over their property, then states (which have acquired much of their territory through unjust wars, colonization, and fraudulent treaties) cannot be regarded as the legitimate owners of their territories. Consequently, they lack the right to bar entrance to outsiders. In fact, if a given national community has illegitimately taken away a piece of territory from another community, then as compensation it *ought* to let in members of the latter, and allow them to establish residence there. Moreover, if a community supports another community's policy of rights violations (for some foreign policy reason), such as persecution on religious or political grounds, then the former owes it to the victims of such regimes to provide them with a safe haven. Note, though, that in so far as, according to libertarians, individuals do not owe material assistance to one another, they do not owe it to economic migrants, or even to economic refugees, as it were, to grant them entry into their community. Only those whose rights of self-ownership are being violated by their own state with the complicity and help (be it indirect help) of host communities are owed safe haven by the latter. In sum, libertarianism would seem to mandate open borders, at least *prima facie*, as a way to rectify past injustices – just as some commentators have argued, you recall, that it also allows for coercive taxation as a way to compensate the worst off for breaches of the Lockean proviso.

We shall address the issue of compensation for past injustices in greater detail in chapter 7. Meanwhile, and for the sake of argument, let us assume that entitlements are legitimate. In that scenario, Steiner's cottage analogy suggests that a political community can decide, without moral restrictions, to bar entry to foreigners, *however serious their need*. For to the extent that, according to libertarians, one is not under an obligation of justice to help others meet their needs, not even their basic needs, one is not under an obligation to grant them asylum. To coerce individuals so to act would constitute a violation of their rights of ownership over their property – again, on the assumption that one's holdings are legitimate.

And yet, the libertarian position as deployed by Steiner is not as clear-cut as it seems. In his example, the community has the right to veto the sale of a cottage by one of the members if the cottage is to be sold to an outsider. However, it does not have the right to veto *visits* of outsiders to community members: I cannot sell you my cottage, but I can surely invite you to stay at my place for as long as I want. By the same token, while I, as a citizen of a wealthy country, cannot singly confer on you all the privileges of membership, I can nevertheless invite you in: others – by extension, my government – cannot keep you out. Nor can it prevent you from working for me if we so agree. As we saw in chapter 1, if someone rightfully owns a resource, then he ought to be able to transfer it to someone else without interference. Thus, if someone rightfully owns a certain amount of money, he ought to be able to give it to his visitor (in our example) in exchange for labour. The point has considerable practical relevance. In effect, it rules out the very stringent restrictions which many (rich) countries place on people who want to come and visit their relatives, or who do not seek to settle permanently in the host country but to work there for a while, only to go back to their home countries once they have had a chance to improve their, and their family's, economic situation.

Those considerations bring out a difficulty inherent in extending extremely individualistic principles such as libertarian justifications for private property to collective ventures. The libertarian is saying the following: 'a state is made up of individuals who each have legitimate entitlements over a piece of territory. Those individuals join their properties together, and form an association which exercises rights over the collective territory, as it were, so constituted. Those decisions are legitimate if, and only if, they violate neither the self-ownership rights of individual members nor their ownership rights over material resources.' The problem, of course, is that decisions regarding the state's territory, and most notably decisions as to whether or not to allow foreigners in, are made collectively. In order for those decisions to violate neither the self-ownership nor the world-ownership rights of individuals, they must secure the consent of all. Now apply this requirement to the issue of immigration. Suppose that I want to bring some would-be immigrants over to my country. Suppose further that my fellow community members want to prevent them from entering the country, on the grounds, for example, that those newcomers do not share our culture. If the decision is made by each of us singly, I have, in effect, a right of veto over others' preference, with the effect that these foreigners are allowed to enter our territory. This is tantamount to violating my fellow members' ownership rights over our territory, since they cannot decide that these individuals will be excluded.

Suppose, by contrast, that we have agreed, prior to making this particular decision, that such issues would be settled by majority voting. In that case, *my* ownership right over the territory would be violated. In other words, there is no way, once collective decisions are at issue, to respect everybody's ownership rights *on each and every occasion*.

The foregoing argument invites an obvious reply from the libertarian, namely that we all consent to the use of a procedure for making such decisions. So we consent, in advance, to not being able to decide whether a specific person or group will be allowed in. As we have given such consent in advance, if the decision goes against us, we cannot really complain that our rights of ownership have been violated. But the difficulty, of course, is that, once the libertarian makes that concession, she has to accept that such a decision-making procedure will yield other results to which she objects, such as coercive taxation for helping the poor. It is hard to see how she can complain, in such cases, that taxation for those purposes violates individual rights of self-ownership.

It seems, then, that libertarians are faced with a number of difficulties when modelling their account of immigration on their accounts of private property. In addition, they are not committed to the view that political communities can do whatever they wish with respect to immigrants.

5 Who should take in immigrants?

As I noted at the outset, it is one thing to say, as some do, that wealthy countries are under an obligation to grant foreigners access to their territory and, in so doing, to confer on them some of the benefits of membership. It is quite another to ascertain who, exactly, should fulfil that duty. Discussing in detail how those countries should allocate that duty among themselves is somewhat beyond the scope of this chapter. Of course, one may take the view that individuals who have a claim to be allowed into another community ought to be able to choose where they will end up living. It is not clear, however, that this should be so, simply because host countries cannot let in everyone who wishes to come in, and because other individuals might have a stronger claim to settle there. Thus, it seems plausible to hold that would-be immigrants who already have close relatives, such as a spouse or children, in a given host country have a greater claim to migrate to this particular country than someone who has no such prior tie there.

Setting aside cases of families, the principle of compensation, to which I have already alluded here, furnishes us with another way of devolving the task of taking immigrants in. Thus, former colonial powers could take on members of their former colonies, as reparation for the ills which (it is assumed) have befallen the immigrants' countries as a result of colonization. Likewise, wealthy countries which are guilty of the most serious wrongdoings vis-à-vis would-be immigrants (by not sending them aid, for example, or by supporting their oppressive governments) would take a greater share of individuals from those particular countries. More generally, pre-existing ties between a host and a home country would identify the former as a natural haven, as it were, for the latter's would-be emigrants.

Let us assume, then, that countries all have to admit a certain number of immigrants every year, on a quota basis. This view has led some philosophers to wonder whether they ought to be allowed to trade those quotas among themselves. The proposal is as follows. Each country has to take in a certain percentage of the total number of world refugees and immigrants, with quotas to be defined by taking a variety of criteria into account, such as GNP per capita, population density, etc. These quotas would also be exchangeable in part or in total, so that a country which would be unwilling to take on its fair share of refugees would be allowed to pay another country willing to take more refugees than the latter's quota imposes. A trade in refugee quotas would thus follow.

This proposal for allocating refugees and immigrants among host countries is based on a similar proposal for pollution quotas, whereby countries who wish to pollute more than they are allowed buy pollution shares from countries which are willing to pollute less. The total yearly pollution remains the same, but is distributed on the basis of willingness and ability to pay. As applied to immigration, the proposal gives host countries a measure of control over whom they take in, and whom they do not, and thus the ability to preserve their cultures from outside influences. It is likely to be met favourably by libertarians and some communitarians. On the other hand, and precisely for this reason, it will be met with scepticism by liberals who do not wish to enable countries to buy their way out of liberal principles. Moreover, some might see general ethical problems about buying one's way out of burden-sharing: consider, for example, criticisms as levelled against the ancient practice, prevalent in some countries in the nineteenth century, whereby the scions of wealthy families were able to pay destitute young men to do their military service in their place. Finally,

exchanging and trading immigration quotas may go against the interests of the immigrants, who may end up in countries where they have
no family, no relatives, etc. To be sure, that they have a right of entry
may not mean that they have a right to go wherever they want. Still,
there might be limits to how much, and where, they can be moved
around. At the very least, any such scheme would have to take those
factors into account, so that not all immigrants would be subject to
those trade-offs.

6 Conclusion

In this chapter, we have looked at various positions on immigration.
We have attempted to articulate coherent Rawlsian and more generally
egalitarian liberal lines on the issue, and assessed both a communitarian and a libertarian approach. Understanding what immigration
controls actually involve, namely undermining freedom of movement,
or denying membership in a given community, has been crucial to our
inquiry. We have also seen that whichever stand one takes on immigration depends, in part, on the extent to which one wishes to confer
greater weight on the demands of one's fellow community members
than on the demands of outsiders.

7 Reparative Justice

1 Introduction

In the previous six chapters, we have reviewed what egalitarian liberals, communitarians, and libertarians have to say on two questions: What do we owe to others, and to whom exactly do we owe it? These two questions do not exhaust all that there is to say on justice. In particular, one must address the following issue: What can and ought to happen if an injustice has been committed?

This question in turn divides into two: (a) What can the victim of the injustice do to get redress? For example, can he go to war against the wrongdoer?, and (b) What ought the wrongdoer to do vis-à-vis his victim? In this chapter, we will look at the second of those two issues – the issue, that is, of reparative justice. Although it has attracted growing attention in the academic literature in recent years, compared to the issue of distributive justice it has generated relatively few book-length works (but see Barkan, 2000; Thompson, 2002). And indeed, at first sight, reparative justice seems remarkably straightforward. Suppose I steal your car. Surely I must give it back to you. And if I cannot do so (for example, because I sold it to someone else, or because I destroyed it in a crash) I must give you enough money to buy a similar car. I also owe you compensation for the inconvenience which my wrongdoing caused you.

So far, so simple. But here is a twist. Suppose now that, having stolen your car, I die in a crash. Is my son under a duty to give the car back to you? Certainly. If the car is destroyed in the crash, is he under a duty to pay you compensation, out of his pocket? After all, he is not guilty of the wrongdoing, so why should he pay?

And here is a further twist. Suppose that *you* die in a freak accident (say in a gas explosion) after I stole the car from you but before my son gave the car back or paid you compensation. Is my son under a duty to your daughter to do either? What kind of grievance, in this particular case, can *your* daughter possibly have as a result of *my* wrongdoing?

This is the kind of case which will concern us here: a case, that is, where both the agent guilty of the initial injustice and the victim of that injustice are dead, and where the latter's successors or descendants make a claim for reparation against the former's successors or descendants. Such cases will be our focus because they have been most prominently raised in the academic literature as well as in legal and political contexts. To give but a few examples: in the last thirty years or so, some African Americans have demanded compensation from the US government for the wrong of slavery. Likewise, in New Zealand, some members of the Maori community, who were dispossessed of their land in the nineteenth century by the British crown, have demanded that the land be returned to them. Similar demands have been made by the Sioux, both for restitution of their land and for compensation for harm done, against the US government. Some of the descendants of the victims of the Nazi regime (as well as those victims themselves) have also demanded compensation for the harm done to their ancestors in the Holocaust, as well as restitution of property stolen from them.

Those claims have sometimes been met with some degree of success. Thus, in 1980, the US Supreme Court awarded the Sioux the sum of $122 million as compensation for the US government's violation of the treaty whereby, in 1868, the Sioux had been guaranteed protection of their territory. In 1992, the High Court of Australia held that the appropriation of native land by British settlers since the beginning of colonization was unlawful, on the grounds that autochthonous tribes, contrary to settlers' and the crown's assumption, did have a pre-existing system of ownership law. Similarly, the German government has paid out compensation to Holocaust victims and their descendants. On the whole, though, the successors of the alleged wrongdoers have been very reluctant to pay up. They have shown greater willingness to issue apologies for their predecessors' actions. Queen Elizabeth II has apologized for Britain's exploitation of the Maoris in the nineteenth century. King Juan Carlos I of Spain has apologized for the expulsion of Jews from Spain in 1492. Pope John Paul II also asked for forgiveness for all the sins committed by the Catholic Church for the last two thousand years.

The foregoing remarks help shape the agenda for the forthcoming discussion. Three questions present themselves to us. On what grounds, if any, are *victims' successors* owed anything? On what grounds, if any, do *wrongdoers' successors* owe anything to victims' successors?

What, exactly, is owed? When answering those questions, we will have to bear in mind four different distinctions.

First, so far I have spoken of victims' and wrongdoers' descendants and successors. In the literature, the term 'descendants' is standardly used. However, we must distinguish between two senses in which currently existing individuals are victims' or wrongdoers' descendants. In the strict sense, a currently existing individual may be the grandson of someone who was wrongfully dispossessed of her property during, say, the Second World War, or the granddaughter of the agent who was guilty of this wrongdoing. In a looser sense, a currently existing individual may be the successor, as it were, of the victim or wrongdoer: not a member of their family lines, but someone who belongs to their group. Thus, the son of a German Jew whose family heirlooms were taken away from her before she was deported to Auschwitz might demand reparations against the descendants of the individual who committed the act if he is known. Alternatively, she might demand reparations against currently existing, non-Jewish Germans, via the German state, not because they are the wrongdoers' descendants, but because they belong to the community of non-Jewish Germans, which extends over time, and some of whose members were guilty of the wrongdoing. Conversely, an African American might demand reparations against the US government, on the grounds that *his* ancestors were dispossessed of their rightful property and grievously wronged. Alternatively, he might demand reparations on the grounds that, as an African American, he belongs to a community some of whose members (and not necessarily *his* ancestors) were grievously wronged by slavery and its legacy. As we shall see, some justifications for reparations work better when claimants and claimees (if I may be granted this neologism) are the descendants, in the strict sense, of victims and wrongdoers. I shall use the term 'descendants' to describe individuals who belong to the initial victims' and wrongdoers' family line, and the term 'successors' to describe individuals who belong to the same community as initial victims and wrongdoers. I shall also use the terms 'claimant' and 'claimee' to denote the specific roles of each. Conversely, I shall use the terms 'ancestors' and 'predecessors' when working backwards, as it were, from the present to the past.

Second, we must distinguish between reparation by way of *restitution* (giving back the very same property or territory which was taken away), reparation by way of *compensation* (giving the monetary equivalent of that which was taken away as well as giving money for the harm done), and reparation by way of *symbolic public gestures* (remembrance ceremonies, public apologies by heads of state, etc.). Certain kinds of wrongdoing may call for restitution (as when territorial rights have been violated), whereas others cannot but call for compensation (it would not make sense for the descendant of someone who died at Auschwitz to ask for restitution as reparation for her parent's death). In this chapter, we will focus on restitution and compensation because they may impose considerable costs on claimees, and are therefore harder to justify than apologies, which come cheap (even though leaders, for political reasons, have been reluctant at times to issue them).

Third, we must distinguish between injustices which consist in the wrongful taking of property and territory, and injustices which consist in violations of what one may call personal rights, such as the right not to be killed, the right not to be unjustly imprisoned, the right not to be raped, etc. I shall sometimes refer to those injustices as injustices, or wrongs, done to the person. As we shall see, some justifications for reparations work better for the wrongful taking of property or territory than they do for violations of personal rights.

Fourth, we must distinguish between reparative claims made by *nations*, such as the Maoris and the Sioux, and reparative claims made by individuals for harms done to their individual ancestors or predecessors. Typically, the former are demands for the restitution of the territory from which the nation was unjustly expelled, whereas the latter are demands for restitution of unjustly taken private property as well as compensation for the attendant losses and/or violations of personal rights. African Americans' demands for compensation for slavery, or Jews' demands for compensation for the Holocaust, are paradigmatic examples of individual claims. To be sure, black people were held in slavery, and Jews were slaughtered, for belonging to a group – in that instance, a particular ethnic group. However, to return to a point made in section 2 of chapter 4, we must differentiate between goods which are valued by individuals as such (such as their own survival, for example, or their bodily integrity) and goods which are valued by individuals in so far as they belong to a group (such as national self-determination). Unjustly taking away the former might be classified as an individual wrongdoing, whereas unjustly taking away the latter might be regarded as a communal wrongdoing. As we shall see, some arguments in favour of reparation for communal wrongdoing do not work well with reparation for individual wrongdoing, and vice versa.

One final remark before I begin. A full theory of reparative justice should assess the weight of reparative principles relative to other principles of justice. Suppose, for example, that a country is under a duty to give substantial reparations to a nation whose rights it has violated in the past. Suppose further that honouring its reparative obligation would jeopardize the provision of basic resources to its current members. Whether or not it is, *all things considered*, under a duty to do so, is a very difficult issue which I will not address here. Rather, I will focus on various approaches to reparative justice taken alone.

2 Egalitarian liberalism and reparative justice

As we have seen throughout this book, egalitarian liberals are divided on the question of what, exactly, we owe to one another. Thus, luck egalitarians argue that inequalities for which individuals are not responsible are unjust, and warrant redress. By contrast, for suffic-ientists, justice merely requires that all individuals have enough resources, and allows substantial inequalities above and beyond the sufficiency threshold. In the context of international justice, then, luck egalitarians are more likely to subscribe to radical cosmopolitan views, and in particular to deny that national borders are morally significant. Sufficientists, on the other hand, tend to be less hostile to the view that borders do matter from a moral point of view. Unsurprisingly, we find similar differences between those strands of egalitarian liberalism when we examine their positions on reparative justice. In section 2.1, I first outline luck egalitarian and sufficientist points on reparations. As we shall see, they offer limited justification for this practice. In section 2.2, I discuss four egalitarian liberal justifications for repara-tions which do not explicitly appeal to either luck egalitarianism or sufficientism.

2.1 Luck egalitarianism, sufficientism, and reparations
Luck egalitarianism Let us start with the luck egalitarian take on repa-rations. Reparations, you recall, may involve either giving back pro-perty which was taken unjustly (restitution), giving the victim the monetary equivalent of that property (compensation), or offering money to make up for the harm done to her (compensation again). Moreover, reparations can be, and are, claimed by nations and indi-viduals. Interestingly, luck egalitarians are unlikely to be sympathetic to those demands. Consider, first, reparative claims made by nations. As we saw in chapter 5, to the extent that they are committed to luck egalitarianism at a global level, luck egalitarians deny that national

borders are ethically significant. Consequently, a nation cannot claim reparation for harm done to it in the past. Suppose, for example, that nation A and nation B are separated by a lake rich in natural resources. Suppose further that, two hundred years ago, A and B made a treaty whereby they agreed to share those resources equally. Suppose, finally, that A has consistently violated that treaty by forcibly preventing B from mining the lake's bed. B now argues that it has been the victim of a historic injustice; and it insists that A restitute its section of the lake's bed, as well as offer compensation for the loss of the wealth which B would have been able to extract from the lake had A not acted unjustly. At the bar of luck egalitarian justice, nation B has no claim against A. This is because the fact that those two nations happen to be located next to a resource-rich lake is morally arbitrary, and neither of them, therefore, has any particular claim to those resources. In fact, luck egalitarians might even say that, to the extent that nations A and B did not share those resources with the rest of the world, their treaty was unjust to begin with.

To return, then, to some of the cases I mentioned at the outset, the luck egalitarian will query the legitimacy of restitutive and compensatory claims made by the Sioux against the US government and by Maoris against New Zealand on grounds of territorial injustice. Interestingly, she will also query the legitimacy of some of the reparatory demands made by African American individuals against the US government. An important justification for African Americans' claims for compensation goes like this. Their ancestors, it is claimed, were forced to work for nothing on plantations. Had they been treated as free individuals, and had they been offered a wage for their labour, they would have acquired wealth which they would have then passed on to their descendants. The latter, therefore, have been unjustly deprived of their rightful inheritance, and the US government ought to give it back to them, with interest (Kershnar, 1999).

There are many difficulties with this kind of argument, some of which I shall highlight in section 4 below. Its central weakness, from a luck egalitarian point of view, is that it presupposes that inheritance is legitimate. But, for the luck egalitarian, inheritance is very problematic. Imagine two generations, G1 and its descendant G2. Some members of G1 will pass on wealth to their children, whereas other members will instead decide to spend their entire wealth before they die. As a result, some members of G2 will be better off than others. Clearly, those inequalities between two individuals who belong to generation G2 and which are consequent on intergenerational transfers of resources from G1 to G2 are a matter, for the worse off, of bad brute luck – namely the brute luck of not having inherited anything. To put the point differently, those who, in G2, are worse off as a result of not having inherited anything from G1 are not responsible for their predicament, and the luck egalitarian cannot condone this state of affairs. The implication for the inheritance argument deployed by African Americans, or for claims made by the descendants of Jews whose property was stolen from them by the Nazis, is straightforward. To the extent that those claims depend on the view that inheritance is legitimate, they fail, precisely because, as far as the luck egalitarian is concerned, inheritance is unjust.

To be absolutely clear: the luck egalitarian does not deny that a grievous injustice was done to Sioux, African Americans, or Jews. She fully accepts, for example, that although the Sioux lacked territorial rights over the land which they occupied, the forcible expulsions and massacres of which they were victims were a serious injustice, and did call for compensation of the victims by the wrongdoers. Likewise, she fully accepts that, although descendants of slaves do not have inheritance rights in the wealth which their ancestors would have created had they been paid for their labour, slavery itself is a paradigmatic example of injustice, and called for compensation by wrongdoers to their victims.

However, what she denies is that those nations, and those individuals, are owed restitution of that piece of land on the grounds that territory and property that belonged to them was unjustly taken away from them. Moreover, her main concern is with *present* inequalities between Sioux and white people, or African Americans and white people, irrespective of the fact that those groups' and individuals' ancestors or predecessors were, respectively, victims and wrongdoers. Thus, she might recommend giving back to the Sioux their ancestral land – not because they had a right to it to begin with, but because giving them the land might be the best practical way to redress current inequalities between the Sioux and white Americans. She might also recommend that white Americans give billions of dollars to the successors of enslaved African Americans (note: not to their *descendants* as such), not because the latter have a historical right to it, but as the best way to redress existing inequalities between African Americans and white Americans.

Sufficientism   Sufficientists will hold a somewhat different view on those various reparatory demands. For a start, as we saw in chapter 5, although they too argue that, from the point of view of what we owe as a matter of justice, national borders are irrelevant, they accept that, once our obligations have been met, they are relevant. Let us return to our earlier example, involving a treaty made by nations A and B with regard to a lake rich in natural resources. According to sufficientists, provided that A and B meet their obligations to ensure that individuals from other states have enough, they are entitled to hold on to the surplus wealth which they create. Any treaty which they conclude and which is compatible with their obligations to other non-nations is therefore legitimate. Consequently, if A breaches B's rights by violating the treaty, it owes restitution and compensation to B. This argument, note, applies whether or not claimants belong to the same family lines as the initial victims of the injustice, and whether or not claimees belong to the same family lines as the wrongdoers.

Furthermore, sufficientists can endorse the institution of inheritance, provided that those who do not stand to inherit anything are not left below the sufficiency threshold. Accordingly, there is nothing incoherent, from a sufficientist point of view, about claims for reparation which appeal to the inheritance entitlements of victims' descendants.

2.2 Refining the position

As I have just suggested, both luck egalitarians and sufficientists can agree that slave-holders and perpetrators of genocide owed compensation to their victims. They can also agree that those such as the Sioux and Maoris who were dispossessed of land to which they did not have a rightful claim were owed compensation by wrongdoers for the unspeakably violent manner in which they were treated. Difficulties arise, however, when reparations are claimed by the descendants or successors of those Sioux, slaves, or Jews against the descendants or successors of the wrongdoers. As we saw, the luck egalitarian can offer a pragmatic reason for compensation as the best way to remedy current inequalities, but will not justify those demands by invoking a past injustice. The sufficientist, for her part, can appeal to the institution of inheritance, but could not thereby justify compensation for crimes against the person. The question, then, is this: are there any backward-looking, egalitarian liberal justifications for reparations for historical wrongdoings which can cover both restitution and compensation, and explain why wrongdoers' descendants or successors owe reparation to victims' descendants or successors?

In this section, I outline four such arguments, all of which consist, in some way, in connecting historical wrongs with the present. They are egalitarian liberal in that (a) they regard the individual as the fundamental locus of moral norms, (b) do not confer on groups, such as nations, moral standing above the standing of their individual members, and (c) subscribe to the view that individuals all have equal moral status. Moreover, in so far as they ground the obligation to offer reparations for the past in what is happening in the present, they overcome a standard objection to reparative claims, namely that, on principle, they have no time limit. According to the objection, a wrong is a wrong whether it was committed yesterday or 1000 years ago. To say that past wrongs warrant reparation, then, is to say that the descendants or successors of the Normans owe reparation to the descendants or successors of Anglo-Saxons for the invasion by the former of the latter's land, England, in 1066. This, however, is absurd, not least because one simply can no longer identify and distinguish those two communities. Reparative obligations, in other words, tend to fade over time (Waldron, 1992). The views we are examining here all take this point on board, since they all advert to a feature of the present to justify both restitution and compensation.

Victims' descendants are still suffering from the wrong As we saw at the outset, a justification for reparations for an injustice which was committed in the distant past must show why victims' descendants or successors are owed anything. The most straightforward argument to that effect claims that those individuals are themselves suffering from the injustice – in effect, that they too are victims. As Randall Robinson has argued in the context of reparations for slavery, the effects of an injustice can be felt for a long time after the injustice has been committed, and by those who were not even born when it was committed (Robinson, 2000).

It is important to distinguish between two variants of the argument. On the first variant, claimants argue that they have been harmed by the past injustice itself. For example, someone born in 1950 to Auschwitz survivors but whose entire extended family was wiped out in the Holocaust, and whose upbringing was marred by her parents' trauma, may plausibly claim that she herself was harmed by the Holocaust. On the second variant, claimants argue that the initial injustice for which they are claiming compensation triggered further injustices from which they are suffering today. This, in fact, is at the heart of the demands made by some African Americans. The problem, they claim, is not so much slavery, but slavery's legacy, which is one of continuous injustice, beginning a decade or so after the Civil War with legally sanctioned segregation in the South and informal but persistent discrimination in the

North. As some commentators have noted, in order to identify exactly the harms from which claimants are suffering, and what they are owed if anything, one must identify the injustice for which reparations are claimed – in this case, slavery, or the segregationist laws, or subsequent acts of discrimination post the Civil Rights movement of the 1950s and 1960s (Bittker, 1973).

Assuming that one can identify that injustice, the view that claimants are owed reparations because they themselves are victims needs qualifying. Strictly speaking, if present harm is the reason why reparations are owed, then one need not be a *descendant* of an initial victim in order to qualify. An African American whose ancestors came to the USA from Ghana in 1920 may suffer from slavery and its legacy – simply in virtue of being black – even though his ancestors were never enslaved.

With this qualification in place, this justification for reparations still faces two difficulties. First, it must establish that claimants have indeed been harmed by the initial injustice and/or by the chain of further injustices which it triggered. Second, even if they have been harmed by those injustices, it must show that their current predicament is mostly due to them.

Two arguments are standardly deployed against the view that claimants have been harmed by the initial injustice. The first one is raised specifically in the context of reparations for slavery. It points to the differences between the levels of social and economic well-being enjoyed by black people in the USA and those enjoyed by black people in Africa, and holds that, as the former have more opportunities and a higher standard of living than the latter, they cannot complain that they would have been better off if their ancestors had not been sent to the New World. The problem, with this argument, is this. It assumes that the relevant comparison is between a hypothetical state of affairs where the ancestors of current African Americans never left Africa, and the state of affairs that actually obtained, where they were shipped to America and held in slavery. However, another, more relevant comparison would be between the state of affairs that obtained, and one where those individuals left Africa *and* were treated as free human beings and paid for their labour (Butt, forthcoming). Under *that* comparison, current African Americans can plausibly argue that they are the victims of a historic injustice.

The second argument is the non-identity objection, which we encountered in chapter 2. According to the objection, current generations do not have obligations to their distant descendants to (for example) preserve the environment, since conservationist policies would result in the non-existence of those descendants themselves. In the context of reparations, the objection holds that victims' descendants have no claim at the bar of justice, since, had the initial injustice against their ancestors not taken place, they would not exist (Wheeler, 1997). Thus, had the Maoris not been dispossessed of their ancestral land by the British crown, they would have, at the time, led a very different life, met different sets of people, and had sexual intercourse at different times and with different partners from those with whom they did, eventually, mate. Genetically different Maoris would currently exist, and existing Maoris therefore cannot complain that *they* have been harmed by the initial injustice.

Now, as we saw in chapter 2, the non-identity objection assumes that assessing whether someone has been harmed, and thus wronged, requires assessing the quality of their life overall. However, and to reiterate, the fact that someone has not been harmed overall by a particular act does not preclude the possibility that he has been harmed along a particular dimension. Thus, even if existing Maoris have not been harmed overall by the act of dispossession of which their ancestors were victims, they may nevertheless have been harmed by it, and by successive unjust acts, along a particular dimension, such as lower educational and economic opportunities than non-Maoris.

Even if the argument under scrutiny here manages to overcome the non-identity objection, it must show that the predicament in which current victims find themselves (for example, poverty) can be traced directly to the injustice for which they claim reparation, and is not of their own doing. But that is quite hard to show. Suppose that, forty years ago, an African American student was denied a place at law school on the grounds of race. Instead of trying again a year later, that student became despondent, neglected his studies, settled for less than he could have achieved, and as a result did not enjoy as high a standard of living as he would have done. There is no doubt that his situation can be explained in part by the injustice which he suffered. But there is equally no doubt that it can also be explained in part by the choices which he made in reaction to that injustice (Sher, 1981). It may be, then, that he is owed some compensation, but any claim for it would have to take on board the extent to which he is responsible for his predicament. Likewise, any claim made by current victims would have to take on board the extent to which they are responsible for their predicament. Interestingly luck egalitarians are likely to be particularly sympathetic to this qualification to reparative claims, since they believe that individuals ought to be held responsible for their choices.

Claimees are still benefiting from the wrong The foregoing justification for reparations focuses on victims' descendants and successors. But even if they are owed reparation, establishing that *wrongdoers'* descendants and successors are under the corresponding obligation requires further work. A standard argument to that effect invokes the fact that claimees are still benefiting from the wrong done by their ancestors or predecessors. In so far as they are the beneficiaries of that wrong, the argument goes, they owe restitution or, as the case may be, compensation – for both crimes against persons and crimes against property. Take the case of slavery. In the early days of the colonization of the New World by Europeans, slavery met the need of these new colonies for a cheap and abundant labour force. Ships filled with goods (such as rum) would sail from Europe to Africa, where those goods would be exchanged for slaves (usually captives in internecine local wars). Slaves would then be sent to the New World (under appalling conditions) where they would be sold, at a sizeable profit, and forced to work on plantations (thus producing cotton, molasses, and so on). The products of their labour would be sold, again at a considerable profit, to European populations. Cities such as Liverpool and Bristol in England and Nantes and Bordeaux in France, whence the ships began on their journeys, lived off the slave trade for close to 200 years. More generally, the wealth generated by the so-called triangular trade filled the coffers of the British, French, and Portuguese states, and gave American capitalism a solid foundation (Thomas, 1997). On some accounts, it is fair to say that denizens of those countries are still benefiting, 200 years on, from the effects of the trade, simply because they are still benefiting from the institutions (economic, educational, scientific, etc.) which were established and funded from its proceeds. In addition, the argument sometimes goes, in the USA, white people are also benefiting, not merely from slavery itself, but also from the decades of discrimination which African Americans have endured as a result of slavery. Had African Americans been given the same social and economic opportunities as white Americans, the latter would not enjoy such a secure and dominant position in American society.

As the example makes clear, the 'benefiting from the past' argument supposes that, just as claimees are benefiting from past injustices, claimants are still suffering from it. We examined that view above.

For now, let us assume, for the sake of argument, that claimees are indeed still benefiting from the injustice, and assess what this entails. Note, firstly, that this defence of reparations need not apply exclusively to wrongdoers' descendants. For just as not everyone who suffers from a past injustice is a descendant of an initial victim of that injustice, not everyone who benefits from it is a wrongdoer's descendant: thus, a white American of Italian descent whose ancestors set foot in New York in 1920 may still be benefiting from slavery and its legacy.

Note, secondly, that the defence applies both to individual and to communal wrongdoings. For what matters for establishing that victims are owed reparations is that some individuals, here and now, are still benefiting from the past wrongdoing. Whether the wrong was done to individuals or to groups of individuals is, in this case, irrelevant.

Moreover, the argument, if it justifies anything, does not justify reparation for stolen property, be it restitution of the property itself or reparation by way of its exact monetary equivalent. In those cases, it is the mere fact that something was unjustly taken away from its rightful owner which supports the demand for reparation. Whether or not claimees are still benefiting from the theft is irrelevant. It might be thought relevant, however, to demands for compensation for harms suffered by individuals in their person (such as slavery and genocide), as well as for harms suffered by them as a result of the loss of their property. Take the Maori case. Although they are demanding the restitution of their ancestral territories in New Zealand, they might conceivably make a compensatory claim on the grounds that, as a result of the initial act of unjust dispossession, they, as a community, are still suffering from a number of social and economic ills (racial discrimination, higher unemployment and imprisonment rates than non-Maori, etc.). And they might conceivably argue that the reason why non-Maori New Zealanders ought to compensate them for *those* harms is that they, nowadays, are still benefiting from the past.

However appealing the 'benefiting from the past' defence seems, it faces a problem which, for some philosophers, is insurmountable, namely that it imposes burdens on present beneficiaries for enjoying benefits which they did not voluntarily accept. A denizen of Bordeaux in France may indeed greatly enjoy his town's architectural beauty and cultural heritage, and be aware that they were funded by the proceeds of the triangular trade. Yet he might complain that there is no reason why he should pay compensation to present victims, since those are public goods which he has no choice but to enjoy: after all, he can hardly avoid walking past the grand buildings which were built by slave traders.

Whether or not one can be held liable for costs for benefiting from a good which one did not voluntarily accept is a hotly contested issue, particularly in the literature on positive discrimination. Some philosophers claim that voluntary acceptance is not a necessary condition for having to compensate those who provided that good in the first instance (Thomson, 1986). Others, by contrast, and unsurprisingly libertarians, maintain that it is a necessary condition (Fullinwider, 1975; Nozick, 1974). But, as others have noted, casting the issue in all-or-nothing terms (either compensation is due, or it is not due at all) is unhelpful, as it overlooks a third option, whereby those who benefit from a past injustice owe something to victims, albeit not necessarily full compensation (Butt, 2007).

Claimees are still guilty of injustice towards victims' descendants   We have just examined one justification for the claim that claimees are under an obligation to give reparations to victims' descendants or successors. That justification appeals to the fact that the former are still benefiting from the injustice. In this section, we assess another justification for reparations, which rests on the claim that claimees are themselves wrongdoers. This interesting argument runs as follows (Butt, forthcoming; Sher, 2005). Individuals generally are responsible for the wrongdoings committed by their nation on their behalf, even if they have not themselves directly taken part in those wrongdoings. Suppose that nation A acts unjustly towards nation B at time t – for example, it takes from B a piece of land, L, which it had promised, by way of a treaty, not to seize. A is clearly under an obligation to return L to B, but defaults on it. At time t_1, a year after the injustice occurs, A clearly is still under an obligation to restitute L to B. In addition, it owes B compensation for the harm resulting from the injustice. However, the composition of A will have changed in the meantime: some members of A who took part in the initial injustice are now dead; others who were not able to participate in the decisions leading up to the injustice are now full members of A. Thus, to claim that A is under a duty of reparation to B at t_1 is to accept that individuals who were not wrongdoers at t are nevertheless wrongdoers at t_1 for failing to give reparation to B. Quite obviously, the argument works over time, so that the overlapping generations which make up A at t_1 will in part survive into t_2 and, together with a new generation, make up A at t_2. Likewise, the overlapping generations which make up A at t_3 will in part survive into t_4, and so on, *ad infinitum*.

This justification for reparations, which applies to both communal and individual wrongdoings, has three key features. First, it rests on the fact – obviously true but generally overlooked in discussions of intergenerational justice – that generations overlap with one another. Suppose that they did not, so that no member of nation A who exists at t also exists twenty-five years later, at t_{25}. If that were the case, then it is harder indeed to justify holding A at t_{25} under any obligation whatsoever to nation B, since no member of A would have had any role in the initial injustice or in his ancestors' or predecessors' failure to compensate B. Second, whether or not A still benefits from the initial injustice at, say, t_{200}, is entirely irrelevant to its reparative obligations. What is relevant is that, over time, A has been continuously derelict in its obligation, since it has continuously failed to restitute L to B, *and* to compensate B for its persistent failure to compensate it. Third, A owes reparations to B if, and only if, the latter is suffering from the former's persistent dereliction of duty.

Whether or not this defence of reparations can overcome the non-identity objection is an interesting question (Butt, 2006). More worrisome, perhaps, is its reliance on the view that individuals are collectively responsible for what their nation does in their name. Many acts of historic injustice were committed by states who were not in any way democratic. Many failures to compensate victims for these initial injustices are also those of non-democratic states. In so far as individual members of those states have no say either in the initial injustice or in subsequent derelictions of reparative duty, it is hard to discern why, exactly, they owe compensation to claimants. It seems, then, that this argument for reparations supports only a handful of claims. Still, it would support claims made by African Americans against the US state for the wrongs done to them by slavery and subsequent failures to compensate them. It would also support similar claims as made by Maoris against the New Zealand state, or, indeed, by populations of countries which were colonized in the nineteenth century by, say, France and Britain. (Having said that, the fact that those countries did not give the right to vote to women – in other words, to half of their adult population – until the late nineteenth century at the very earliest does raise doubts as to their democratic character when the initial injustice and the first failures to compensate took place.)

The liberal transgenerational community and reparations The final egalitarian liberal argument in defence of reparations which I want to examine here has been put forward by Janna Thompson in her important book on reparative justice (Thompson, 2002). As applied to reparation for wrongs done to nations or national communities, it appeals to the notion of transgenerational community. We encountered that notion in chapter 2, when discussing de-Shalit's communitarian view of obligations to future generations. According to him, human beings belong to a community of moral values, language, culture, history, and traditions, which persists over long periods of time, and which is the source of our obligations to our successors (de-Shalit, 1995). As we shall see in section 3 below, a similar account of the transgenerational community underscores a communitarian justification of reparations. But Thompson's account of the transgenerational community is somewhat different. In a nutshell, if we want to bind our successors, we have to accept that we are bound by our predecessors. For when we bind our successors, for example by concluding a treaty under the terms of which we promise not to seize land from an aboriginal community, we accept a central feature of this practice, namely that reparations will have to be paid by our successors if we breach that initial commitment. And if we expect our successors to offer reparations for *our* failure to honour those commitments, then we must be prepared to offer reparations for our ancestors' failure to honour *their* commitments.

Note that the argument applies not merely to reparations for wrongs against national communities, but also to reparations for wrongs done to individuals. In the latter case, it appeals to the notion of family lines. Individuals, Thompson argues, are members of families who are bound together by blood ties over time. As family members, most notably as parents, we have a vested interest in making plans and developing goals, for the sake of our children, which will only be realized once we are dead. Those goals are typically of two kinds: they pertain to the disposal of our property and to the transmission, to our children and grandchildren, of our values and culture. We thus have a strong interest in binding our successors to respect our wishes regarding our property and children. In particular, we have a strong interest in binding our successors to respect our children's inheritance rights, as well as to preserve our family line. In so doing, we accept that others may have a similar interest in their immediate descendants' welfare. We also accept the practice of offering reparations for failure to honour inheritance rights and to preserve family lines, and we thus place our successors under an obligation to offer reparations for our own such failures. This, in turn, means that we have to accept that we are bound by what our ancestors

did, and have to offer reparations for their failure to honour their contemporaries' inheritance rights and to preserve their family lines.

Thompson's justification thus supports compensation for stolen
property. It also supports compensation for wrongs such as slavery
and genocide, in so far as they destroy family lines. This is so not
simply for the obvious reason that they result in the destruction of
families through the death of their members, but also because they
are severely disruptive of familial relationships, and thus impair the
processes of communication through which parents pass on their
values and culture to their children.

As the foregoing points suggest, compensation claims, on
Thompson's view, are limited in time. For in order to make her case
successfully, a victim must show that she is the heir of a victim who
was dispossessed unjustly, or that she is a member of a family line
which was unjustly destroyed and that, as such, she is still suffering
some harm. The more time has elapsed between the initial injustice
and the claim for compensation, the less likely it is that claimants
could demonstrate either fact.

Thompson easily accepts this implication of her argument.
However, she might find it harder to deal with the following criticisms
(Miller, forthcoming). First, her justification for reparations assumes
that our successors ought to offer compensation and/or restitution to
the descendants of our victims. But whether or not they are under
such an obligation is precisely the point at issue. It is hard to see, then,
how she can avoid the charge of begging the question.

Second, not all wrongs done to nations are treaty violations. Had
white settlers forcibly expelled the Sioux from their ancestral land in
the absence of a treaty, they would also have been guilty of wrongdoing. Thompson's argument for reparations to nations does not cover
this particular case. Instead, she claims that nations which deserve
respect must treat one another with respect. This entails that they
must not wrong each other (for example by taking each other's territory) and that, if they are guilty of such wrongs, they must then offer
restitution, compensation, or both, as a way to restore mutual respect.
As she herself notes, however, restoring mutual respect need not
require reparations; it may be done by making it clear that one will
treat other nations with respect from now on. In other words, there is
no deep connection between reparations and ensuring that nations
treat one another with respect.

Finally, Thompson's defence of reparations for lost inheritance is
more problematic. We saw in section 2.1 that luck egalitarians are

unlikely to accept this particular defence of reparations, precisely in so far as it regards inheritance as legitimate. In section 4, we will discuss further difficulties with inheritance- and bequests-based justifications for reparations. For now, let us turn to communitarian views on reparations for historic injustice.

3 Communitarianism and reparative justice: a mixed view

As we shall see in this section, communitarianism lends itself to two very different accounts of reparations for past injustice. Some communitarian thinkers develop an understanding of the transgenerational community which allows for reparation. On some other communitarian views, however, reparations are problematic in so far as (the argument goes) they rest on the view that what past generations did was unjust, and thus illicitly impose the present generation's principles of justice on their ancestors and predecessors.

3.1 The communitarian transgenerational community: in defence of reparations

As we saw in chapter 2, some philosophers of communitarian leanings justify the claim that we have obligations to our successors by appealing to the notion of transgenerational community. But their account of such a community is rather different from Thompson's. For Thompson's view does not appeal so much to the importance of long-term values and traditions as to the importance, for a community, of being able to bind its successors for the sake of its goals and projects. And whereas Thompson's voluntaristic account speaks of obligations which one imposes on oneself precisely by imposing similar obligations on others, the communitarian account of the transgenerational community speaks of duties which one does not choose to incur. The following statement, from McIntyre's *After Virtue*, powerfully captures what those communitarians have in mind:

> I am born with a past; and to try to cut myself off from that past, in the individualistic mode, is to deform my present relationships. The possession of an historical identity and the possession of a social identity coincide . . . What I am, therefore, is in key part what I inherit, a specific past that is present to some degree in my present. I find myself part of a history and that is generally to say, whether I like it or not, whether I recognize it or not, one of the bearers of a tradition . . . [Practices] always have history and . . . at any given moment what a practice is depends on a mode of understanding it which has been

transmitted often through many generations. And thus, insofar as the virtues sustain the relationships required for practices, they have to sustain relationships to the past – and to the future – as well as in the present. (McIntyre, 1981, p. 221)

We do find here a basis for reparative obligations. For if I am born with a past, and if my identity is shaped by my past, then I cannot deny that past, on pain of denying who I am. Moreover, if my present, *social* identity is shaped by my past, indeed by my community's past, then I must accept that my relationships with others cannot but be shaped by that past. Thus, if I am a white American, I cannot, on pain of denying who I am, ignore the historical fact of slavery, and I have to accept that my relationship with contemporary African Americans is influenced by it. If I am a German gentile whose family lived in Germany during the 1930s and through the war, I cannot, on pain of denying who I am, brush aside the Holocaust, and I have to accept that my relationship with Jews is influenced by it. As McIntyre himself puts it,

the Englishman who says, '*I* never did any wrong to Ireland; why bring up that old history as though it had something to do with *me*?', or the young German who believes that being born after 1945 means that what Nazis did to Jews has no moral relevance to his relationship to his Jewish contemporaries, exhibit the same attitude, that according to which the self is detachable from its social and historical roles and statuses. (McIntyre, 1981, pp. 220–1)

And elsewhere:

A central contention of the morality of patriotism is that I will obliterate and lose a central dimension of the moral life if I do not understand the enacted narrative of my own individual life as embedded in the history of my country. For if I do not so understand it I will not understand what I owe to others or what others owe to me, for what crimes of my nation I am bound to make reparation, for what benefits to my nation I am bound to feel gratitude. Understanding what is owed to and by me and understanding the history of the communities of which I am a part is on this view one and the same thing. (McIntyre, 1995, pp. 224–5)

Here, McIntyre criticizes modern individualism and, by extension, contemporary, Rawlsian liberalism. As we have seen, though, contemporary liberals have mounted arguments for reparations which do rest on the claim that current generations cannot ignore their past. Their main point of divergence with McIntyre on this issue pertains to the extent to which individuals, here and now, are *constituted* by their collective past. McIntyre and communitarians who are sympathetic to his views believe that they are – so that, for example, a German born after 1945 *cannot* identify himself as German unless he acknowledges that the Holocaust is an inherent part of German-ness. And perhaps, as applied to this particular example, McIntyre is right. Quite obviously, though, his understanding of our relationship to our past, and the justification for reparations that may emerge from it, is vulnerable both to the passage of time and to the changing composition of communities. To be sure, egalitarian liberals also face that difficulty, which is why they seek to connect the past injustice to a present injustice. But the problem raised by the passage of time is more acute for someone such as McIntyre. For the further back one goes into the past, the less important past practices, values, and institutions are to our identity. To what extent, for example, must a Spaniard, as a Spaniard, regard the expulsion of Jews from Spain in 1492 as part of his identity? Moreover, the further one goes into the past, the more likely it is that our societal culture over time is made up of conflicting practices and values. Thus, legally entrenched discrimination against women was a pervasive and essential practice in most European cultures until very recently. It no longer is: gender equality is the norm, albeit one that is not always adhered to. What, then, shapes the identity of contemporary Europeans? We encountered that problem – of time passing – in chapter 2. There, we asked whether we could plausibly justify obligations to distant successors by appealing to the notion of a transgenerational community, given that future generations' communities are likely to be very different from ours. Here, it is apt to ask whether we can plausibly justify obligations towards the descendants and successors of victims of injustice when the injustice was committed such a long time ago that we cannot identify with that past community.

3.2 Judging the past: a very limited defence of reparations
Interestingly, though, one can be a communitarian and altogether reject the idea of reparative obligations, or at the very least endorse them in far fewer cases than egalitarian liberals and communitarians such as McIntyre would be prepared to accept. In chapter 1, you recall, we saw that, according to some communitarians, most notably Sandel and Walzer, justice is not universal in scope. As Walzer powerfully puts it, 'Justice is rooted in the distinct understandings of places, honors, jobs, things of all sorts, that constitute a shared way of life. To override those understandings is (always) to act unjustly' (Walzer,

1983, p. 314). At first sight, though, it seems that the very idea of reparative justice goes against Walzer's particularistic understanding of justice, at least when the wrong for which reparation is sought was committed in the distant past. For to say that claimees owe reparation to claimants is to imply that the former's predecessors and ancestors acted wrongly, *even if they themselves believed that what they were doing was right*. In other words, reparative justice requires judging the past by the present's standards. In Walzerian terms, it involves violating the shared social meanings of our ancestors, and thereby failing to respect the latter as producers of such meanings.

Any argument against reparations which appeals to a Walzerian account of justice in particular, and to cultural relativism in general, presupposes that cultural relativism and *historical* relativism are the same phenomenon, so that past periods of time are as different from one another as cultures. This, of course, raises some difficult issues of delineation. In particular, it is hard to see what counts as a 'cultural period', when such a period starts, and when it ends (Butt, forthcoming). Assume, though, that this problem can be solved. One must then distinguish between radical and moderate variants of this communitarian argument against reparations. On the radical view, we, here and now, can *never* make a moral judgement on past actions, any more than we can make a moral judgement on cultures other than ours. As a result, reparations are never owed by anyone to anyone. Discussing this view would require discussing extreme moral relativism *per se* – a task which is far beyond the scope of this book. One obvious problem with extreme moral relativism is that it is vulnerable to itself, as it were. If our moral beliefs are necessarily relative to those whose beliefs they are, and if it is impossible to make any external moral judgement on anyone or any act, then presumably the belief that *this* is how we should think about morality is itself relative, and there is no principled reason, therefore, to endorse it.

A more interesting view on reparations which is also inspired by cultural relativism holds that reparations are owed only in a handful of cases, and in far fewer than may be supposed. This, in fact, appears to be Walzer's view. Although *Spheres of Justice* deploys what seems to be, on the face of it, a radical form of cultural relativism, Walzer also stresses that there are certain things that a community cannot do to its members if it is to be regarded as a community. It is on this ground that he condemns Britain's failure to take steps first to avert and then to alleviate the potato famine which devastated Ireland in the nineteenth century. Moreover, in his book *Thick and Thin*, he insists that there are moral universals which hold in the overwhelming majority of cultures, such as the prohibition on murder, betrayal, and deception (Walzer, 1994). Finally, he also claims that to respect individuals as producers of social meanings is to respect their rights to collective self-determination, which entails that colonization is therefore unjust (Walzer, 1995).

It seems, then, that Walzer would be able to endorse, at least on principle, the view that Britain owes compensation to Ireland for the famine; the view that Germany owes compensation to victims of the Holocaust and their descendants; and the view that restitution and compensation is owed by colonial powers to the countries which they invaded, and dispossessed of their land, in the eighteenth and nineteenth centuries. Upon closer scrutiny, however, matters are not so straightforward. Note, first, that this account of reparations would justify compensation and restitution only for the most serious kinds of injustice. In fact, above and beyond the threshold set by those thin moral universals, deeds performed by our ancestors and predecessors (or, for that matter, our culturally different contemporaries) could not count as unjust unless they were regarded as such at the time. Needless to say, this is a view which egalitarian liberals would find difficult to endorse. Take the case of the rape of women, for example. It may well be true that it has almost always been prohibited, by almost all cultures. But it is not true that it has always been regarded as a wrong done *to* the victim. The view that it is a wrong done to her family or her husband has always been prevalent, and still is in many parts of the world. Likewise, and for related reasons, the view that, in war, raping women is either an acceptable means of warfare, or a just reward for the victors, has also been prevalent. This example is particularly apposite in the context of this chapter. During the Second World War, about 200,000 women from all over South-East Asia were coerced into sexual slavery by the Japanese army. Those women, some of them girls as young as twelve, were raped repeatedly (as well as beaten and tortured) over long periods of time by Japanese soldiers. Many of them died of internal injury, or became infertile; all endured a lifetime of pain and shame (Yoshimi, 2002). In the mid-1990s, the Japanese government apologized for the wrong done to those so-called comfort women, and set up a privately funded organization, the Asian Women's Fund, which distributes 'atonement money' to victims. Tellingly, however, Japanese governments have resisted survivors' demands for full, publicly funded compensation. To those who believe that more should be done by the Japanese for those women (and for those of their children and grandchildren who have been severely affected by their parents' traumatic wartime experience), Walzer's view does not seem to offer much with which to go on.

More problematically still, even if it is true that almost all societies have prohibited wanton murder, there has always existed wide dis-agreement as to who belongs to the category of those who ought not to be murdered wantonly. Likewise, there has always been disagreement as to who counts as a community member and ought to be treated as such. More widely, there has always been disagreement as to who counts as a producer of social meanings. Six decades ago, a sizeable number of Germans believed that Jews did not meet the criteria for immunity from wanton murder and for community membership. A century and a half ago, a sizeable number of Britons did not regard the Irish as fellow community members either, even though Ireland was under the jurisdiction of the British crown. Two centuries ago, and indeed until recently, colonial powers did not subscribe to the views that American Indians or, for that matter, Africans were producers of social meanings whose collective will warranted respect. In other words, treating community members in particular ways and abstain-ing from wanton murder may well be universals, in that they are to be found in pretty much all communities: more specific, fine-grained accounts of those universals clearly are not. The problem, for Walzerian accounts of reparations, is that we can decide whether victims' descendants are owed reparation by wrongdoers' descendants only if we are given such an account, for the simple reason that we need to know who was a victim, and who was a wrongdoer.

4 Libertarianism and reparative justice

So much, then, for communitarian lines of argument on reparative justice. In this section, we shall turn finally to libertarian justifications for both compensation and restitution. According to Nozick, you recall, a theory of justice comprises three principles: a principle of acquisi-tion, a principle of transfers, and a principle of rectification. According to this, violations of individuals' self-ownership rights, or of their rights over the products of their labour, call for compensation or, as the case may be, restitution. As Nozick himself notes, in so far as no cur-rently existing individual or group, it is fair to say, is the legitimate owner of the resources it commands (who has ever respected the Lockean proviso?), the practical implications of the principle of rectifi-cation are mind-boggling. In effect, our system of ownership rights ought to be abolished, so as to give proper reparations to those who were unjustly dispossessed of their rightful property. At this point Nozick throws his hands up in despair, and concedes that there is space, after all, for the difference principle. We can safely assume – he claims – that victims of injustice are worse off than they would have been otherwise, so that there is a high probability that the worse off, here and now, are the victims of past and present injustices. In so far as the difference principle seeks to improve the situation of the worse off, it can function as a principle of rectification (Nozick, 1974).

Nozick is undoubtedly right that no one, in fact, is a legitimate property-owner (at least, as far as material resources are concerned). He is also right that trying to offer reparations to all those who have a legitimate claim to them would be practically impossible. Still, assessing the principle of rectification within a libertarian framework is worthwhile. For if the principle is misguided, then we will not be able to endorse the difference principle as its best approximation. Put differently, if the normative basis for Nozick's practical concession is unsound, then this concession needs a different justification.

The principle of rectification calls for restitution of stolen property, as well as compensation for the harms suffered as a result of that initial injustice. It also calls for compensation for violations of self-ownership rights. In addition, it applies not merely to individual wrongdoings, but also to injustices done to groups such as nations. As we saw in chapters 4 to 6, libertarians see no difficulty whatsoever in individuals forming political associations with jurisdiction over a particular territory, if that territory is made up of those individuals' legitimately and privately owned holdings. Consider, thus, the violation by the US government of the treaty they concluded in 1868 with the Sioux – a treaty in which they undertook to guarantee the protection of the latter's ancestral territory. Assume, for the sake of argument, that the Sioux were the legitimate owners of that land. Early violations of the treaty, when individuals who signed it on both sides of the conflict were still alive, straightforwardly did call for restitution and compensation from a libertarian point of view.

As ever, though, difficulties arise when reparative demands are made by victims' descendants against wrongdoers' descendants. Note, first, that, within a libertarian framework, reparations are justified by appealing to inheritance and bequests. This implies that claimants are entitled to reparations not because they are the successors, as community members, of initial victims, but because they are their rightful heirs. More often than not, heirs are also family members, which is why I shall refer to them as 'descendants'.

Now, take reparations for stolen property (such as artworks stolen from Jews by the Nazis) or for wrongfully taken territory. To claim that the former are entitled to reparations, either in the form of restitution or in the form of compensation, is to assume that they are in fact the rightful owners of the property. But there are two ways in which someone's descendant can become the rightful owner of her property upon her death. Either the deceased has bequeathed the property to him; or he is entitled to inherit it. As we saw in chapter 2 when discussing justice towards future generations, libertarians usually endorse the choice-based theory of rights whereby, in order to have a right, one must be able to demand or waive the performance of the corresponding duty. In so far as the dead are not in a position to do either, they simply cannot have rights (Steiner, 1994). In other words, in the choice-based theory of rights, there is no such thing as a right to bequeath property. This entails that victims' descendants cannot claim to have a right to the property which their ancestors would have bequeathed them had the initial injustice not taken place.

Of course, as we also saw in chapter 2, libertarians can endorse the interest-based theory of rights. But even on that view, it is unclear that there can be a right to bequeath property. For rights, in the interest theory, protect interests, and any account of a right to bequeath must therefore provide an account of whose interest it protects. Whether or not the dead, being dead, can have interests at all remains a contested issue. If they cannot, then there is no such thing as a right to bequeath, which in turn vitiates reparative demands made by victims' descendants on those grounds.

The latter might do better to claim, therefore, that, even if their ancestors did not have the right to bequeath their property in the first instance, they nevertheless have the right to inherit it. Even so, they would face a number of challenges. First, as David Lyons argues in an important article, inheritance claims are not apposite when reparations for the violations of territorial rights are at issue. As he puts it in the context of Native Americans' claims,

> A tribe is a continuously existing entity, like a nation, that spans the relevant generations of human beings. The land was originally held in common by the tribes, and that is how the land would be recovered . . . Its ownership [of a territory by a tribe] need not be thought of as involving transfer from one individual to another by inheritance or any other means. (Lyons, 1982, p. 364)

According to Lyons, thus, a community's rights over its territory are not simply the concatenation of community members' individual rights over their land. We encountered a similar criticism when discussing the libertarian position on immigration in chapter 6. Assume that this criticism is misguided. Still, as Lyons further argues, the institution of inheritance is problematic, not merely for egalitarian reasons given in section 2.1 above, but for *libertarian* reasons as well. In so far as inheritance results in the concentration of wealth, and therefore of power, into the hands of a few, it enables the latter to impose their will on the many who have not inherited anything. Put bluntly, inheritance facilitates unfair bargains and agreements, and thus 'promotes injustice in transfer' (Lyons, 1982, p. 365).

A second major difficulty with inheritance-based arguments for reparations is that they seem to regard property rights as immune to changing circumstances. Nozick himself concedes that our property rights change if, for example, other people become unable to feed themselves as a result of some sort of catastrophe. One way in which circumstances change is through the arrival of newcomers. So it may be that Native Americans were the rightful owners of the land; it may also be that the institution of inheritance is, in principle, justified. Even then, whether or not the descendants of the Native Americans who were dispossessed of their land have a claim to it depends on the extent to which we must take into account the arrival of hundreds of thousands of emigrants to the USA since the dispossession took place. Even if Native Americans had not been dispossessed of their land, their descendants, a generation later, might have had to relinquish part of it anyway, so as to allow new settlers to acquire property rights in it. If so, current descendants of Native Americans would not have a claim to that land (Lyons, 1982; Waldron, 1992).

Note, however, that some libertarians dispute that the problem of changing circumstances is as acute for their theories as it is often thought to be. On their view, the inhabitants of a territory must relinquish a fair share of it to make place for waves of newcomers, but they can choose which part of the territory specifically to relinquish. Moreover, should they fail to give newcomers a fair share, the latter can seize it by force, but cannot just take whatever share they want. Properly specified, then, historical property rights can change, without simply fading away, which in turn enables them to accommodate restitutive demands (Simmons, 1995).

A third difficulty, for the inheritance justification, is its use of counterfactuals. It claims that, *if* the initial dispossession had not taken place, then victims' descendants would now own the property, since they would have inherited their ancestors' entitlements in the property. So *if* the Jewish owner of a Picasso painting had not been unjustly dispossessed of it, she would have retained an entitlement in it, which she would have passed on to her grandchildren. In so far as they are its rightful owner, the argument goes, the painting should be returned to them. As we saw in section 2.1, a similar argument is sometimes deployed in support of African Americans' demands for compensation for the fact that their ancestors were never paid for their labour. And a similar argument could be made in support of restitution and compensation for the wrongful loss, by a nation, of its territory.

However, those claims face two obvious challenges. The first one is posed, once again, by the non-identity problem. If the initial dispossession had not taken place, those individuals who are now making a reparative claim would not have existed, and it is not true, therefore, that *they* would have stood to inherit from their ancestors. What is the libertarian to make of this? She could concede that the challenge is powerful when raised against reparative claims for individual wrongdoings. Against communal wrongdoings, she might be tempted to claim that it has no bite, for it *is* true that, had the initial injustice not taken place, the current generation of victims' descendants, as a generation and irrespective of the genetic identity of its members, would have stood to inherit. Note, however, that a libertarian will find this response to the challenge difficult to reconcile with his overarching theory of group rights. Suppose that, at time t, the group enjoys a collective right over a piece of land, L. This right is the concatenation of the group members' individual rights over parcels of L. At time t_1, the group is wrongfully dispossessed of the land. That is to say (for the libertarian), all its members are wrongfully dispossessed of their parcels. At time t_{10}, the victims' descendants claim that they are owed compensation and restitution on the grounds that, as a group, they would still be in possession of the land if the injustice had not taken place. That may well be true. But according to the libertarian, the collective right which the group would have enjoyed at time t_{10} but for the initial injustice is the concatenation of the individual rights which the group members would have had over parcels of L at that time. If so, then it must be the case that those group members would indeed have had those rights. And yet, that cannot be the case, precisely because *they* would not have existed had the initial injustice not taken place.

Even if, as some have argued, inheritance arguments for reparations are not troubled by the non-identity problem (Kershnar, 1999), they must deal with another challenge, namely, how do we know? How do we know that the initial Jewish owner of the Picasso painting would still have had a rightful title to it upon her death? After all, she might have sold it, in which case she would no longer have had any entitlement to it – an entitlement, therefore, which her descendants would not have inherited. Likewise, how do we know that African Americans in the nineteenth century would have held on to their earnings, instead of spending them, and thus losing their entitlement to them? How do we know that a Maori tribe, who was unjustly dispossessed of its land, would *not* have sold it, at a fair price, to some settler (Waldron, 1992)? We simply do not know – and the more time has elapsed, the harder it is for us to reach such judgements. Some theorists of reparative justice remain unconvinced by this objection, and reply that we make counterfactual judgements all the time, and use them as the basis for allocating blame, praise, and liabilities. Provided that we are conservative in our judgements (for example, we assume, reasonably, that people on the whole tend not to act rashly or impulsively), then, 'in the absence of full knowledge of what would have occurred had a wrong not been committed, blaming a wrongdoer conservatively constitutes a fair compromise between assuming that his wrong would have had horrible consequences for the wrong party and assuming that his wrong would have had wonderful consequences' (Simmons, 1995, p. 158; see also Thompson, 2002).

Whether or not counterfactual reasoning can provide a useful guide for assessing reparative demands remains a contested issue. Resolving it is beyond the scope of this book. Instead, let me end this study of libertarians' justifications for reparations with the following point. As you will have noticed, the discussion has focused on reparative demands for wrongfully taken property. It has not said much at all about reparative demands for violations of personal rights. The reason for that is very simple. According to the libertarian, to violate someone's self-ownership rights (for example, by killing or enslaving them) is an injustice for which compensation is owed to the victim. Unlike property rights, however, self-ownership rights are not inheritable by the owner's descendants. As a result, descendants of Holocaust victims or of enslaved African Americans cannot demand compensation for the crimes against the person to which their ancestors were subjected. To many, this might be a serious limitation of libertarian justifications for reparations.

5 Conclusion

In this chapter, we looked at arguments for reparations which challenge the two-pronged view that only the victims of the initial injustice are owed reparation and that only wrongdoers themselves owe it
to them. As we saw, all three schools of thought, except the luck egalitarian strand of egalitarian liberalism, advocate reparations, although
some of them find reparations for the wrongful taking of property and
territory much easier to justify than reparations for violations of personal rights. Be that as it may, they all (again, except luck egalitarianism) accept that victims' descendants are owed reparations as a matter
of justice, and thus broaden the scope of justice across generations.

8 Conclusion

We began this book by noting that a theory of justice defends a particular view of what is owed to whom. In other words, it delineates both the content and the scope of those obligations. As we saw, traditional accounts of justice until fairly recently have argued that, whatever is owed (an equal distribution, or a distribution according to needs), it is owed mostly by citizens to their fellow contemporary citizens, via the institutions of a territorially bounded sovereign state.

As we also saw, however, those traditional accounts have been challenged from a number of directions: by globalization, by the fact of ethnic and cultural pluralism, and by a growing awareness of the claims which our successors might make on us, as well as of the claims which our contemporaries make on us on the grounds that their ancestors suffered an injustice. Justice, in other words, must be sensitive to cultural, religious, and ethnic differences between citizens of territorially bounded states. Moreover, it extends across space, and over time. In this book, we reviewed those challenges through the lenses of three dominant theories of justice, namely egalitarian liberalism, communitarianism, and libertarianism.

I will not summarize our findings here. Instead, I should like to outline further avenues for inquiry. The theories of justice which we examined here all offer normative responses to our changing world. Although the topics I have selected are among the most important of the changes which we have been witnessing for the last thirty years, normative thinking on justice cannot stop here and now. It must turn its attention to cultural, economic, social, and technological shifts the implications of which are far from clear. To give but two, headline-grabbing examples, climate change on the one hand and biotechnologies on the other hand are affecting us, and will affect our children and grandchildren, in ways which we cannot quite fathom yet. Notwithstanding this epistemic difficulty, it is imperative that we begin to think about what to do in those areas, and it is therefore crucial that we devise normative principles upon which to base our decisions. I do not know what those principles are. I do not know yet, for example, what libertarians can say about genetically modified food, what communitarians can say about climate change, or what egalitarian liberals can say about the genetic engineering of human beings. But the fact that all three theories, in one way or another, have been able to deal with our changing world so far is testimony to their intellectual health and dynamism. There is little doubt that their fundamental tenets and principles will prove useful guides for exploring those relatively unchartered territories.

References

Al-Hibri, A. Y. (1999). 'Is Western Patriarchal Feminism Good for Third World/Minority Women?', in J. Cohen, M. Howard and M. Nussbaum (eds), *Is Multiculturalism Bad for Women?* Princeton, NJ: Princeton University Press.

Anderson, B. (1991). *Imagined Communities: Reflections on the Origin and Spread of Nationalism.* 2nd edn, London: Verso.

Anderson, E. (1999). 'What is the Point of Equality?', *Ethics* 109, 287–337.

Arneson, R. (1989). 'Equality and Equality of Opportunity for Welfare', *Philosophical Studies* 56, 77–93.

—— (1993). 'Equality', in R. E. Goodin and P. Pettit (eds), *Blackwell Companion to Political Philosophy.* Oxford: Blackwell.

Barkan, E. (2000). *The Guilt of Nations: Restitution and Negotiating Historic Injustices.* New York: Norton.

Barry, B. (1992). 'The Quest for Consistency: A Sceptical View', in B. Barry and R. E. Goodin (eds), *Free Movement: Ethical Issues in the Transnational Migration of People and Money.* London: Harvester Wheatsheaf.

—— (1999). 'Sustainability and Intergenerational Justice', in A. Dobson (ed.), *Fairness and Futurity: Essays on Environmental Sustainability and Social Justice.* Oxford: Oxford University Press.

—— (2001). *Culture and Equality: An Egalitarian Critique of Multiculturalism.* Cambridge: Polity.

Beckerman, W., and Pasek, J. (2001). *Justice, Posterity and the Environment.* Oxford: Oxford University Press.

Beiner, R. (1998). 'National Self-Determination: Some Cautionary Remarks Concerning the Rhetoric of Rights', in M. Moore (ed.), *National Self-Determination and Secession.* Oxford: Oxford University Press.

Beitz, C. (1988). 'Recent International Thought', *International Journal* 43, 183–204.

—— (1999). *Political Theory and International Relations.* 2nd edn, Princeton, NJ: Princeton University Press.

Bell, D. (1993). *Communitarianism and its Critics.* Oxford: Oxford University Press.

Beran, H. (1984). 'A Liberal Theory of Secession', *Political Studies* 32, 21–31.

Berlin, I. (1969). 'Two Concepts of Liberty', in *Four Essays on Liberty*. Oxford: Oxford University Press.

Bittker, R. (1973). *The Case for Black Reparations*. New York: Random House.

Brighouse, H. (2004). *Justice*. Cambridge: Polity.

Brilmayer, L. (1991). 'Secession and Self-Determination: A Territorial Interpretation', *Yale Journal of International Law* 19, 177–202.

Buchanan, A. (1989). 'Assessing the Communitarian Critique of Liberalism', *Ethics* 99, 852–82.

—— (1991). *Secession: The Morality of Political Divorce from Fort Sumter to Lithuania and Quebec*. Boulder, CO: Westview Press.

—— (2004). *Justice, Legitimacy, and Self-Determination: Moral Foundations for International Law*. Oxford: Oxford University Press.

Buchanan, A., Brock, D., Daniels, N., and Wikler, D. (2000). *From Chance to Choice: Genetics and Justice*. Cambridge: Cambridge University Press.

Butt, D. (2006). 'Nations, Overlapping Generations, and Historic Injustice', *American Philosophical Quarterly* 43, 357–67.

—— (2007). 'On Benefiting from Injustice', *Canadian Journal of Philosophy* 137, 129–52.

—— (forthcoming). *Rectifying International Injustice: Compensation and Restitution between Nations*. Oxford: Oxford University Press.

Caney, S. (1996). 'Individuals, Nations, and Obligations', in S. Caney, D. George and P. Jones (eds), *National Rights and International Obligations*. Boulder, CO: Westview Press.

—— (2003). 'Entitlements, Obligations, and Distributive Justice', in D. Bell and A. de-Shalit (eds), *Forms of Justice: Critical Perspectives on David Miller's Political Philosophy*. Lanham, MD: Rowman & Littlefield.

—— (2005). *Justice beyond Borders: A Global Political Theory*. Oxford: Oxford University Press.

Carens, J. (1992). 'Migration and Morality: A Liberal Egalitarian Perspective', in B. Barry and R. E. Goodin (eds), *Free Movement: Ethical Issues in the Transnational Migration of People and Money*. London: Harvester Wheatsheaf.

Casal, P. (2007). 'Why Sufficiency is Not Enough', *Ethics* 117, 296–326.

Clayton, M., and Williams, A. (1999). 'Egalitarian Justice and Interpersonal Comparisons', *European Journal of Political Research* 35, 445–64.

Cohen, G. A. (1989). 'On the Currency of Egalitarian Justice', *Ethics* 89, 906–44.

—— (1995). *Self-Ownership, Freedom, and Equality*. Cambridge: Cambridge University Press.

—— (2000). *If You're an Egalitarian, How Come You're so Rich?* Cambridge, MA: Harvard University Press.

—— (forthcoming). *Rescuing Justice and Equality*. Cambridge, MA: Harvard University Press.

Coleman, J. L., and Harding, S. K. (1995). 'Citizenship, the Demands of Justice and the Moral Relevance of Political Borders', in W. Schwartz (ed.), *Justice in Immigration*. Cambridge: Cambridge University Press.

Crisp, R. (2006). 'Equality, Priority and Compassion', *Ethics* 103, 745–63.

de-Shalit, A. (1995). *Why Posterity Matters: Environmental Policies and Future Generations*. London: Routledge.

Dobson, A. (1998). *Justice and the Environment: Conceptions of Environmental Sustainability and Theories of Distributive Justice*. Oxford: Oxford University Press.

Dummett, M. (2001). *On Immigration and Refugees*. London: Routledge.

Dworkin, R. (1981a). 'What is Equality? Part I: Equality of Welfare', *Philosophy and Public Affairs* 10, 185–246.

—— (1981b). 'What is Equality? Part II: Equality of Resources', *Philosophy and Public Affairs* 10, 283–345.

Fabre, C. (2003). 'Global Egalitarianism: An Indefensible Theory of Justice?', in D. Bell and A. de-Shalit (eds), *Forms of Justice: Critical Perspectives on David Miller's Political Philosophy*. Lanham, MD: Rowman & Littlefield.

—— (2007). 'Global Distributive Justice: An Egalitarian Perspective', *Canadian Journal of Philosophy*, supplementary vol. 31.

Frankfurt, H. (1987). 'Equality as a Moral Ideal', *Ethics* 98, 21–43.

Fullinwider, R. (1975). 'Preferential Hiring and Compensation', *Social Theory and Practice* 3, 307–20.

Gans, C. (2003). *The Limits of Nationalism*. Cambridge: Cambridge University Press.

Gellner, E. (1983). *Nations and Nationalisms*. Ithaca, NY: Cornell University Press.

Gibney, M. (2004). *The Ethics and Politics of Asylum: Liberal Democracy and the Response to Refugees*. Cambridge: Cambridge University Press.

Gilman, S. L. (1999). ' "Barbaric" Rituals?', in J. Cohen, M. Howard and M. Nussbaum (eds), *Is Multiculturalism Bad for Women?* Princeton, NJ: Princeton University Press.

Goodin, R. E. (1992). 'If People were Money . . .', in B. Barry and R. E. Goodin (eds), *Blackwell Companion to Political Philosophy*. Oxford: Blackwell.

Hart, H. L. A. (1955). 'Are There any Natural Rights', *Philosophical Review* 64, 175–91.

Held, D., and McGrew, A. (eds) (2003). *The Global Transformations Reader*. 2nd edn, Cambridge: Polity.

Honig, B. (1999). ' "My Culture Made Me Do It" ', in J. Cohen, M. Howard and M. Nussbaum (eds), *Is Multiculturalism Bad for Women?* Princeton, NJ: Princeton University Press.

Jaggar, A. (1983). *Feminist Politics and Human Nature*. Totowa, NJ: Rowman & Allanheld.

Jones, C. (1999). *Global Justice: Defending Cosmopolitanism*. Oxford: Oxford University Press.

Jones, P. (1999). 'Group Rights and Group Oppression', *Journal of Political Philosophy* 7, 353–77.

Julius, A. J. (2006). 'Nagel's Atlas', *Philosophy and Public Affairs* 34, 176–92.

Kershnar, S. (1999). 'Are the Descendants of Slaves Owed Compensation for Slavery?', *Journal of Applied Philosophy* 16, 95–101.

Kukathas, C. (2003). *The Liberal Archipelago: A Theory of Diversity and Freedom*. Oxford: Oxford University Press.

Kymlicka, W. (1989). *Liberalism, Community and Culture*. Oxford: Oxford University Press.

—— (1995). *Multicultural Citizenship*. Oxford: Oxford University Press.

—— (2001). *Contemporary Political Philosophy*. 2nd edn, Oxford: Oxford University Press.

Locke, J. (1988). *Two Treatises of Government*, ed. P. Laslett. Cambridge: Cambridge University Press.

Lyons, D. (1982). 'The New Indian Claims and Original Rights to Land', in J. Paul (ed.), *Reading Nozick*. Oxford: Blackwell.

McIntyre, A. (1981). *After Virtue*. London: Duckworth.

—— (1995). 'Is Patriotism a Virtue?', in R. Beiner (ed.), *Theorizing Citizenship*. New York: State University of New York Press.

Margalit, A., and Raz, J. (1990). 'National Self-Determination', *Journal of Philosophy* 87, 439–61.

Mason, A. (2000). 'Equality, Personal Responsibility, and Gender Socialisation', *Proceedings of the Aristotelian Society* 100, 227–46.

—— (2006). *Levelling the Playing Field: The Idea of Equal Opportunity and its Place in Egalitarian Thought*. Oxford: Oxford University Press.

Meisels, T. (2005). *Territorial Rights*. Dordrecht: Springer.

Miller, D. (1995). *On Nationality*. Oxford: Oxford University Press.

—— (1999a). *Principles of Social Justice*. Cambridge, MA: Harvard University Press.

—— (1999b). 'Justice and Inequality', in A. Hurrell and N. Woods (eds), *Inequality, Globalization, and World Politics*. Oxford: Oxford University Press.

—— (2000). *Citizenship and National Identity*. Cambridge: Polity.

—— (forthcoming). *National Responsibility and Global Justice*. Oxford: Oxford University Press.

Moore, M. (ed.) (1998). *National Self-Determination and Secession*. Oxford: Oxford University Press.

—— (2001). *The Ethics of Nationalism*. Oxford: Oxford University Press.

Mulhall, S., and Swift, A. (1996). *Liberals and Communitarians*. 2nd edn, Oxford: Blackwell.

Nagel, T. (1989). *Equality and Partiality*. Oxford: Oxford University Press.

—— (2005). 'The Problem of Global Justice', *Philosophy and Public Affairs* 33, 113–47.

Nozick, R. (1974). *Anarchy, State and Utopia*. New York: Basic Books.

Nussbaum, M. (2000). *Women and Human Development: The Capabilities Approach*. Cambridge: Cambridge University Press.

Okin, S. M. (1989). *Justice, Gender, and the Family*. New York: Basic Books.

—— (1999). 'Is Multiculturalism Bad for Women?', in J. Cohen, M. Howard and M. Nussbaum (eds), *Is Multiculturalism Bad for Women?* Princeton, NJ: Princeton University Press.

Parekh, B. (2000). *Rethinking Multiculturalism: Cultural Diversity and Political Theory*. Basingstoke: Macmillan.

Parfit, D. (1984). *Reasons and Persons*. Oxford: Oxford University Press.

Pateman, C. (1989). *The Sexual Contract*. Cambridge: Polity.

Patten, A. (2002). 'Democratic Secession from a Multinational State', *Ethics* 112, 558–86.

Perry, S. R. (1995). 'Immigration, Justice, and Culture', in W. Schwartz (ed.), *Justice in Immigration*. Cambridge: Cambridge University Press.

Pettit, P. (1997). *Republicanism: A Theory of Freedom and Government*. Oxford: Oxford University Press.

Phillips, A. (2004). 'Defending Equality of Outcomes', *Journal of Political Philosophy* 12, 1–19.

—— (2006). ' "Really" Equal? Opportunity and Autonomy', *Journal of Political Philosophy* 14, 18–32.

Philpott, D. (1995). 'In Defence of Self-Determination', *Ethics* 105, 352–85.

Pogge, T. (1992). 'Cosmopolitanism and Sovereignty', *Ethics* 103, 48–75.

—— (1994). 'An Egalitarian Law of Peoples', *Philosophy and Public Affairs* 23, 195–224.

—— (2002). *World Poverty and Human Rights*. Cambridge: Polity.

Post, R. (1999). 'Between Norms and Choices', in J. Cohen, M. Howard and M. Nussbaum (eds), *Is Multiculturalism Bad for Women?* Princeton, NJ: Princeton University Press.

Rawls, J. (1993). *Political Liberalism*. New York: Columbia University Press.

—— (1999a). *A Theory of Justice*. 2nd edn, Cambridge, MA: Harvard University Press.

—— (1999b). *The Law of Peoples*. Cambridge, MA: Harvard University Press.

Raz, J. (1986). *The Morality of Freedom*. Oxford: Oxford University Press.

Robinson, R. (2000). *The Debt: What America Owes to Blacks*. Harmondsworth: Penguin.

Roemer, J. (1995). 'Equality and Responsibility', *Boston Review* 20, 3–7.

—— (1998). *Equality of Opportunity*. Cambridge, MA: Harvard University Press.

Sandel, M. (1984). 'The Procedural Republic and the Unencumbered Self', *Political Theory* 12, 81–96.

—— (1996). *Liberalism and the Limits of Justice*. 2nd edn, Cambridge: Cambridge University Press.

Sen, A. (1992). *Inequality Re-Examined*. Oxford: Oxford University Press.

Shachar, A. (2001). *Multicultural Jurisdictions*. Cambridge: Cambridge University Press.

Sher, G. (1981). 'Ancient Wrongs and Modern Rights', *Philosophy and Public Affairs* 10, 3–17.

—— (2005). 'Transgenerational Compensation', *Philosophy and Public Affairs* 33, 181–200.

Simmons, A. J. (1995). 'Historical Rights and Fair Shares', *Philosophy and Public Affairs* 14, 149–84.

Simon, J. L. (1989). *The Economic Consequences of Immigration*. Oxford: Blackwell.

Singer, P. (1972). 'Famine, Affluence and Morality', *Philosophy and Public Affairs* 1, 229–43.

Squires, J. (1999). *Gender in Political Theory*. Cambridge: Polity.

Steiner, H. (1992). 'Libertarianism and the Transnational Migration of People', in B. Barry and R. E. Goodin (eds), *Free Movement: Ethical Issues in the Transnational Migration of People and Money*. London: Harvester Wheatsheaf.

—— (1994). *An Essay on Rights*. Oxford: Blackwell.

—— (1995). 'Liberalism and Nationalism', *Analysis und Kritik* 17, 12–20.

—— (1996). 'Territorial Rights', in S. Caney, D. George and P. Jones (eds), *National Rights and International Obligations*. Boulder, CO: Westview Press.

Swift, A. (2006). *Political Philosophy: A Beginners' Guide for Students and Politicians*. 2nd edn, Cambridge: Polity.

Tamir, Y. (1993). *Liberal Nationalism*. Princeton, NJ: Princeton University Press.

Taylor, C. (1979a). *Hegel and Modern Society*. Cambridge: Cambridge University Press.

—— (1979b). 'What's Wrong with Negative Liberty', in A. Ryan (ed.), *The Idea of Freedom*. Oxford: Oxford University Press.

—— (1986). *Sources of the Self: The Making of Modern Identity*. Cambridge: Cambridge University Press.

—— (1993). *Reconciling the Solitudes: Essays on Canadian Federalism and Nationalism*. Montreal: McGill–Queen's University Press.

—— (1994). 'The Politics of Recognition', in A. Gutmann (ed.), *Multiculturalism and the Politics of Recognition*. Princeton, NJ: Princeton University Press.

Temkin, L. (1993). *Inequality*. Oxford: Oxford University Press.

Thomas, H. (1997). *The Slave Trade: The Story of the Atlantic Slave Trade 1440–1870*. New York: Simon & Schuster.

Thompson, J. (2002). *Taking Responsibility for the Past: Reparation and Historical Justice*. Cambridge: Polity.

Thomson, J. J. (1986). 'Preferential Hiring', in J. J. Thomson, *Rights, Restitution and Risk*. Cambridge, MA: Harvard University Press.

Unger, P. (1996). *Living High and Letting Die: Our Illusion of Innocence*. Oxford: Oxford University Press.

UNHCR (United Nations High Commission for Refugees) (2006). *2005 Global Refugee Trends: Statistical Overview of Populations of Refugees, Asylum Seekers, Internally Displaced Persons, Stateless Persons, and Other Persons of Concern to the UNHCR*. Geneva: UNHCR.

Vanderheiden, S. (2006). 'Conservation, Foresight, and the Future Generations Problem', *Inquiry* 49, 337–52.

Van Dyke, V. (1995). 'The Individual, the State, and Ethnic Communities in Political Theory', in W. Kymlicka (ed.), *The Rights of Minority Cultures*. Oxford: Oxford University Press.

Waldron, J. (1992). 'Superseding Historic Injustice', *Ethics* 103, 4–28.

—— (1993). 'Can Communal Goods be Human Rights?', in J. Waldron, *Liberal Rights: Collected Papers 1981–1991*. Cambridge: Cambridge University Press.

Walzer, M. (1983). *Spheres of Justice*. Oxford: Blackwell.

—— (1994). *Thick and Thin: Moral Argument at Home and Abroad*. Notre Dame, IN: University of Notre Dame Press.

—— (1995). 'Response', in D. Miller and M. Walzer (eds), *Pluralism, Justice and Equality*. Oxford: Oxford University Press.

Wellman, C. (1995). 'A Defence of Secession and Political Self-Determination', *Philosophy and Public Affairs* 24, 142–71.

Wheeler, S. C. (1997). 'Reparations Reconstructed', *American Philosophical Quarterly* 34, 301–18.

Wiggins, D. (1986). *Needs, Value, Truth*. Oxford: Blackwell.

Williams, B. (1973). 'The Idea of Equality', in B. Williams, *Problems of the Self*. Cambridge: Cambridge University Press.

Wolff, J. (2006). *An Introduction to Political Philosophy*. 2nd edn, Oxford: Oxford University Press.

Woodward, J. (1986). 'The Non-Identity Problem', *Ethics* 96, 804–31.

Yoshimi, Y. (2002). *Comfort Women: Sexual Slavery in the Japanese Military during World War II*. New York: Columbia University Press.

Young, I. M. (2001). 'Equality of Whom? Social Groups and Judgements of Injustice', *Journal of Political Philosophy* 9, 1–18.

Index

Moore, M. 83, 90
Mulhall, S. 15
Muslims 51, 56–8, 59–60, 64, 126

Nagel, T. 14, 103, 105–6
Nantes 144
nation 75, 137–8, 149
nation-state 74, 76, 86
national identity 75, 78, 80–1, 84–5, 88
    as a justification for territorial rights
        83
nationalism 75, 77
nationality
    vs. ethnicity 78
Native Americans 157–8
needs 13, 37, 101, 121, 128
Netherlands 41
New Delhi 114, 121
New York 145
New Zealand 52, 134, 145, 147
non-identity objection 45–50, 142–3,
    147, 159
non refoulement principle 114
Normans 141
Nozick, R. 12, 21–6, 127–8, 146, 155–7,
    158
Nussbaum, M. 13, 38, 101

Okin, S. M. 57
original position 5, 31–2, 98, 117–18
ownership 22–6, 42–5, 54, 65, 89, 90–1,
    110–11, 127–30, 155
    see also self-ownership

Pakistan 52, 113
Palestine (Palestinians) 83–4, 92–4
Parekh, B. 63–5
Parfit, D. 46
particularism 16, 106–8, 153
Pasek, J. 41
Pateman, C. 11
Perry, S. R. 121
Pettit, P. 97
Phillips, A. 6
Philpott, D. 88
Pogge, T. 95, 96, 97, 98–9, 107

Poland (Poles) 74, 126
population control 30, 33–4, 40, 41,
    104
pornography 19
positive discrimination 146
primary goods 3–4, 33
pluralism 20

Quebec 52, 56, 76

Rawls, J. 1–6, 15, 19–21, 31–5, 70, 95,
    98–9, 104–5, 116–19
Raz, J. 13, 42, 78
relativism 153
residence 99–102
responsibility 8–12, 99–101, 103–4
rights
    choice-based vs. interest-based rights
        42–5, 79, 91
    corporate vs. collective rights 86
    language rights 52, 56, 67, 85
    self-government rights 52–5, 79
    special representation rights 52–5,
        67
Robinson, R. 141
Roemer, J. 12
Rushdie, S. 64

Sandel, M. 15–16, 17, 19, 86–8
Saudi Arabia 51, 99
Scorsese, M. 64
Scotland 52
Scottish National Party 74
secession 76–7, 80, 81–2, 89–90
self-determination
    national vs. political 75, 88–9,
        109
self-ownership 22–3, 42, 66, 89, 90, 110,
    128–30, 155, 160
Sen, A. 13, 101
Sher, G. 143, 146–7
Sikhs 51, 56–9, 68
Simmons, A. J. 158, 160
Simon, J. L. 122
Singer, P. 97
Sioux 134, 136, 138, 139, 156

Made in the USA
Middletown, DE
25 January 2018